WASHINGTON ROCK CLIMBS

WASHINGTON ROCK CLIMBS

Jeff Smoot

CHOCKSTONE PRESS

EVERGREEN, COLORADO

Published and distributed by
CHOCKSTONE PRESS, INC.
Post Office Box 3505
Evergreen, Colorado 80439

ISBN 0-934641-12-9

Cover photo:
Keith Lenard on Thin Fingers, Index, by Larry Kemp

WARNING

This is only a guide book. It is merely a composite of opinions from many sources on the whereabouts and difficulties of various routes. It is not an instructional book on mountaineering technique or a substitute for the user's judgement. Rock climbing is a high risk sport and the user of this book assumes full responsibility for his or her safety.

Index General Store and the All-Purpose Duck

CONTENTS

PREFACE

It has been over six years since a major guide to the rock climbing in Washington State has been published, and much has happened in those years. This book's predecessor, Don Brooks' *A Climber's Guide to Washington Rock,* published by The Mountaineers in 1982, was greatly anticipated but, unfortunately, was a disappointment to many. While much of the written information was of value, and the introductory material clearly superior, the illustrations and route descriptions didn't quite mesh, and for climbers unfamiliar with the crags and routes presented, the guide was in many instances almost useless.

Not counting the many guides to "lesser" areas, such as Mount Erie, Static Point, and Tieton River (Yakima) basalt, to name only three, this is Washington's sixth major rock climbing guide. The first, Fred Beckey's *Guide to Leavenworth Rock Climbing Areas,* published in 1965 by The Mountaineers, contains much information that is still interesting — even amusing. It is, however, hopelessly outdated, and of interest only to historians and collectors these days. Beckey, the consummate guide book author, published *Darrington & Index Rock Climbing Guide* in 1976, also by The Mountaineers. This book singled out granite climbing on the west side of the Washington Cascades and provided historical data and very detailed written route information, unlike its rival, *Rock Climbing in Leavenworth and Index.* That book, also published in 1976 by Signpost Publications and written by Don Brooks and Rich Carlstad, used excellent photo overlays and brief route descriptions to produce what has arguably been the finest climbing guide to Washington to date. Thus, Beckey's book was useful for routefinding at Darrington and for historical information (which has been criticized as inaccurate and hastily gathered in an effort to beat the Brooks/Carlstad book to press) but was almost obsolete for Index even as it was published.

Brooks continued to take up the guidebook writing slack where Beckey left off when, in 1982, he teamed with David Whitelaw to produce *Washington Rock,* published by The Mountaineers. Brooks' writing was excellent, and his knowledge of Northwest rock climbing is likely unsurpassed, but the book was nevertheless ill-received. This was largely due to the perceived "poor quality" of the book, especially the route diagrams (described by one disoriented reader as "tapeworms crawling up dung heaps"). One visiting climber, using *Washington Rock* as a guide, thought he had repeated Shriek of the Mutilated at Castle Rock, but had in fact free climbed an old aid pitch on the other side of the crag. And while *Washington Rock* was the first to combine all of Washington's major climbing areas into one guide, a noble effort in itself, some Washington climbers and many visitors were greatly disappointed with the result.

In the interim between *Washington Rock* and this guide, Darryl Cramer and Jeff Smoot offered their *Index Town Walls: A Guide to Rock Climbs including Stevens Pass,* a homemade production (Sky Valley Publications, 1985) which, despite being somewhat crude and hastily produced, became an instant hit. This was mostly because it provided much-needed information on the latest wave of free climbs and aid eliminations at the fastest-growing area in the state. The book was sold out within a few months, and as the authors did not reprint it, the need for new information grew.

Hopefully, this guide will adequately cover rock climbing in Washington. Although initially intended to come out in 1987, delays have set it back well into 1989. However, it is hoped that the extra time and effort will make it a valuable and lasting resource, as well as a starting point for some future masterwork. Also, this guide was originally intended to encompass the entire state of Washington, including points unknown in eastern Washington. Unfortunately, little information was forthcoming out of those areas. In those areas where little development has taken place since *Washington Rock,* it is hoped someone will provide updated route information for future guidebook editions.

As Randy Vogel lamented in his *Joshua Tree* guide, it is difficult to present a "comprehensive" guide when few climbers are willing to volunteer information. The author would like to extend his thanks to the following people for their time, effort, and input: Matt Arskey, Jeff Boucher, Brian Burdo, Darryl Cramer, Greg Child, Greg Collum, Lee Cunningham, Cal Folsom, Chris Greyell, Doug Klewin, Matt Kerns, Dan Lepeska, Greg Olsen and Jim Yoder. Special thanks go to Dona Smoot for her patience in typing numerous manuscript revisions. For those who didn't help this time, comments are welcomed on how to improve the guide, and corrections or updates to route descriptions or diagrams are encouraged. Any input should be directed to the author, care of the publisher.

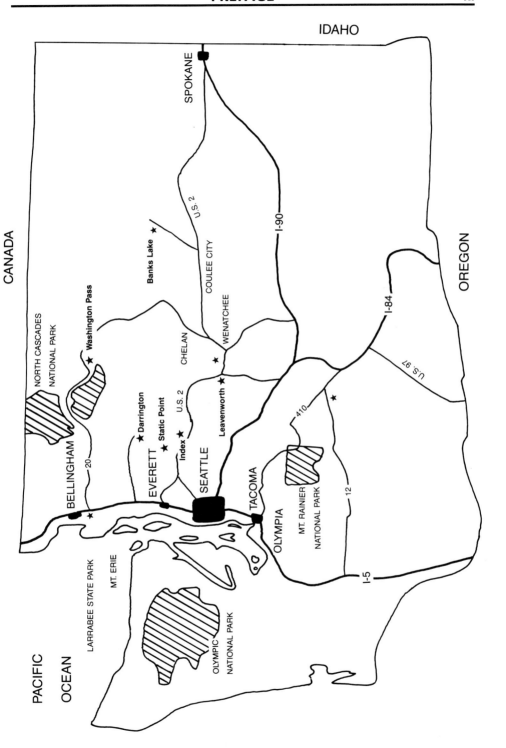

John Stoddard on M.F. Overhang, Castle Rock

INTRODUCTION

Rock climbing in most Washington areas has changed a lot in five years. While some areas have stagnated, other areas are so different that, if you haven't kept up, you've been left far behind. Aid routes have gone free, and yesterday's testpieces are today's trade routes. The sheer number of routes continues to grow, and so far there is no end in sight. Cliffs that were "climbed out" five years ago now have dozens of new climbs. Only a few Washington climbers could lead 5.11 or harder in 1980, and the best usually spent their time in Yosemite; now, it seems, everyone and their dog can climb 5.11, and Index is the place to be – or Smith Rock, for really hard routes. And there are now more 5.12s in Washington than there were 5.11s in 1982. Obviously, something's up.

Climbing development in areas such as Darrington and Peshastin have been difficult to document, Darrington because few admit to climbing there in these days of the 'sport crag', and Peshastin because it has been officially closed since 1986. New areas like Banks Lake, Royal Columns and Mount Erie are being developed by climbers perhaps unwilling to share their pleasures. Therefore, several small and newly developed areas will not be presented here. Those interested in climbing at Darrington hopefully will be able to do so using this guide, but may consider consulting *Washington Rock* for more detailed written route descriptions. Those interested in climbing at Banks Lake should go there and explore, hopefully with someone who has been there before and who has a canoe.

Leavenworth, on the other hand, has had its share of new route activity, and the locals seem to find new routes each year in abundance under the moss and lichen. The major cliffs may be "climbed out", but there are many smaller crags with excellent crack and face lines crying out to be climbed. Also, since the publication of *Washington Rock,* many hard new free climbs have been established and major aid lines freed.

Index has had the most development of any Washington climbing area. Once considered solely an aid climbing area, Index has been transformed into one of the premiere free climbing areas in the country. Aid lines continue to go free, and new lines are forever appearing. There seems to be no end to the number of superb granite crack and face climbs that are discovered at Index each year.

If climbing in Washington is changing, the attitudes about it are not; at least, not as much. While everyone seems a bit more enthusiastic about climbing than they did in the 1970s, Washington climbers are not as rabid as those in other areas, especially about ethics. Routes have always been pre-inspected and pre-protected, hangdogging is nothing new, and bolts are being placed in record numbers. While Washington climbers have tended to be traditionalists in the past, the "new ethics" don't seem too much different than the old. Nobody seems upset when an old aid line that hasn't been climbed since 1982 gets scrubbed, bolted, and led free. This does not mean that everybody agrees; however, much of the remaining unclimbed rock seems to require such tactics. Abundant moss and lichen make on-sight leading of most new routes more than unpleasant, and, as in other areas, blank faces arguably require pre-protection. However, nothing in this guidebook should be misconstrued as "in favor" of any of these techniques for new route production. On the contrary, the issue of bolting, while not yet hotly debated in Washington, is still at issue. Bolts have been chopped and will likely be chopped again. Bolters — especially rappel bolters — should exercise some restraint in new bolt placements. Not every area needs to rival Smith Rock for overbolting, and every route that is climbable does not need to be rappel bolted.

The areas covered in this book are Index Town Walls, Darrington, Static Point, Stevens Pass, Snoqualmie Pass, Tumwater Canyon, Icicle Creek Canyon, Snow Creek Wall, Peshastin Pinnacles, and Liberty Bell/Washington Pass, most of which are located along the two major highways crossing the Cascade Range in Washington — Interstate 90 and U.S. Highway 2. The emphasis will be on Index and Leavenworth, since they are the two most popular rock climbing areas in the state. As such, they will be covered more completely. Many small areas not included in this guide are still being developed, and the author will wait for the developments to become more widely known before printing them. Although geographically situated in Washington, Beacon Rock will not be included; this area is adequately covered in *Oregon Rock*, and is mostly frequented by Portland climbers. Small cragging areas in eastern Washington, including Banks Lake and columnar basalt crags near Yakima will be excluded for now as well.

Though marginally considered a "lowland rock climbing area," Liberty Bell/Washington Pass rock climbs are included in this guide as a matter of convenience to the reader. Fred Beckey's *Cascade Alpine Guide* (vol. III, The Mountaineers, 1981) not only provides route information, photo overlays and some topos, but also geological, historical, and other useful (and useless) information which this guide, for a number of reasons, cannot.

However, as Liberty Bell and its surrounding peaks are generally within an hour's walk from the North Cascades Highway, an outing to Liberty Bell may be no more arduous than one to Snow Creek Wall. Still, the fact that Liberty Bell is a mountain is worth noting; differences in weather, commitment, descent, and preparation should be considered by any parties climbing here.

Perhaps the next edition of this guide will include not only Liberty Bell, but other pure alpine rock routes in other areas, including the Stuart Range, the Enchantments, and the Skykomish River Valley. Such a guide would logically include only the better mountain rock climbs (otherwise, it would be too big), and would likely be of more use to visitors than Washington climbers. However, for now, only Liberty Bell will be included here.

The advent of 5.13 in Washington has brought recognition to this state's rock climbing, but hard or easy, Washington climbing is as good and as varied as anywhere in the world. Most Washington climbers are not climbing at quite that level, but there are abundant 5.6, 5.9 or 5.11 routes to occupy most everyone for the next several years, at least until the next printing of this guide. Perhaps when this guide is finally on the shelves, Washington climbers will be able to discover it for themselves. Rediscover it, that is!

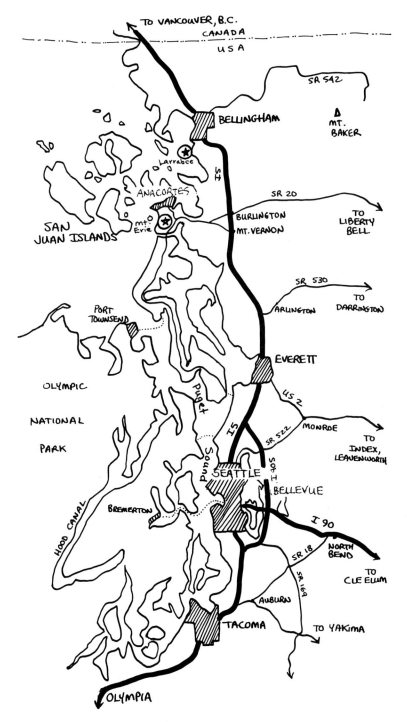

SEATTLE AREA

RATINGS

The ubiquitous and venerable "Yosemite Decimal System" (Tahquitz Decimal System) is used throughout this book. It should require no explanation, but will need a bit of translation.

For the most part, Class 3 and 4 denote unroped scrambling, although a rope may be desireable for some climbers.

Class 5 is subdivided into 5.0 through 5.14 (yikes!), with 5.0 being easy and anything above 5.9 generally being considered hard (although truly hard climbing begins wherever you would consistently fall off).

At 5.10 and above, ratings get complicated by a further alphabetical subdivision, with "a" being easy, "b" being harder, "c" being harder still, and "d" being maximum. Thus, a 5.10a is an "easy" 5.10, while a 5.10d is the maximum difficulty for a 5.10. A word of caution: a 5.10a at Index may seem the same as a 5.10a in Leavenworth, but will usually seem harder than a 5.10a at Squamish or Yosemite. Also, it seems that 5.11's at Index are harder than 5.11's anywhere else. Index ratings have been widely criticized, although the proponents of Index free climbing vigorously defend their ratings. ("5.11's are supposed to be hard," Darryl Cramer insists, trying to convince me that Iron Horse and Japanese Gardens are mere 5.11c's.) In many areas, especially Index, consider the ratings with suspicion, as they may well be off the mark, usually on the low side. The author has tried to compensate for this whenever possible, but may have missed a few. Don't be surprised if you have to back off a 5.10c (that is really a 5.11a).

It is worth noting that the downward trend in free climbing ratings appears as a result of over-familiarity with the routes. As each route is climbed more and more times, those who have climbed a route several times may eventually feel that it is easier than when they first climbed it. This means that, as a pitch is "wired," it will very likely be downrated. However, as this continues, some very difficult routes are trivialized. 5.12's become 5.11's, and too many visiting climbers are "sandbagged." Perhaps a solution would be to grade the routes by their "on sight" difficulty — that is, how difficult it would seem to a climber on his or her first try, or how difficult it is to "flash" the route. In some instances, the author has tried to compensate in this manner. However, in many cases, the rating reflects a consensus rating which has been lowered over the years. So, beware the 5.11b at Index!

Seriousness ratings will be provided as follows:

    PG-13:   Specialized protection required; otherwise, serious fall potential possible. A route with PG-13 may have mild runouts where no protection is possible, but above good protection.

    R: Serious fall potential; questionable or poor protection; serious injury likely.

    X: Death fall potential; very poor or no protection; serious or fatal injury likely.

These seriousness ratings are not intended to be the last word on a route's seriousness, and lack of a seriousness rating does not mean that a route is not serious; climbing is inherently dangerous, and any route is serious for any climber at any time. Routes with seriousness ratings are merely known to be particularly hazardous to the unwary. Any route can be serious if you don't have the right protection or aren't up to the difficulties. The author has tried to warn of dangers when possible, but cannot reasonably be expected to know of every dangerous climb in this guide. What is dangerous to one climber may be perfectly safe for another. There are many other routes which may well be dangerous, but may not be known to be so by more than the few who have climbed them. So, proceed with caution, and at your own risk.

Climbers visiting Darrington and Static Point should be aware that nearly every route there has some type of runout, and thus would be considered R-rated by the standards set forth in this book. The scale is set up to include any runout, whether at the crux, or on easy ground. Thus, if there is a 50-foot runout on 5.6 on a route rated 5.9, that route would receive a seriousness rating (probably an X). The scale is designed to warn of serious climbing, whether easy or hard.

For longer routes, the standard Yosemite (Roman numeral) grading system will be used, whereby a Grade II should take only a few hours, a Grade III half a day, a Grade IV most of a day, and a Grade V can be climbed in one long day by experienced teams, etc. Most people are familiar enough with this system that it need not be elaborated on further. If you don't understand any of this, consult almost any climbing instruction book (John Long's *How To Rock Climb!*, Chockstone Press, 1989, is the best) for the specifics. Again, it is a subjective system. Some climbers may be able to climb two Grade V routes in a day (if they can find two Grade V's in the same area!); others may barely manage one Grade III without bivouacking.

Quality ratings are something new to Washington guidebooks (they were actually introduced to Washington in the 1985 Index guide). The following star system, similar to that used in Joshua Tree guidebooks for many years, is provided:

No stars: Average quality route.
One star (★): Better than average route; worthwhile.
Two stars (★★): Good quality route; recommended.
Three stars (★★★): Excellent route; good position, quality climbing, sound rock; highly recommended.
Four stars (★★★★): Highest quality; should not be missed in this lifetime!

Again, this is a subjective system. Just because a route does not have stars does not mean it is not worth doing. The star ratings are of great help to visiting climbers who may have only a few days to climb in an area before heading on; it provides them with a quick way to determine the quality of a route so they don't spend too much time on "lesser" routes. Also, negative star ratings (e.g., − ★★) are provided to keep everyone off truly unpleasant routes. Negative stars are reserved for routes with bad rock, too much vegetation, or just plain ugly, unaesthetic climbing. Of course, if you are into that sort of thing....

WEATHER

The weather in Washington is probably responsible for the seemingly lackadaisical attitude of most Washington climbers. It always seems to be raining, at least in Seattle in the spring. Leavenworth weather is usually better.

Weather on the west side of the Cascades is usually moist, due to prevailing winds blowing moisture up against the mountains, which seem to get dumped on almost continually between November and June. This accounts for the lush forests and, unfortunately, the abundance of moss and lichen on Darrington and Index granite. After June and until October, western Washington is usually sunny − but don't rely on it! It is a general rule that Mount Erie is sometimes dry when Index is wet, but, again, don't count on it.

Eastern Washington is usually dry, especially Leavenworth, because it sits in a rainshadow created by the Stuart Range. This means that, even if it is raining at Index or Stevens Pass, it may well be dry and possibly sunny at Castle Rock. But, on such days, bringing rain gear may not be a bad idea. During the summer, Index usually has better climbing than Leavenworth, since temperatures in Leavenworth can exceed 100 degrees Farenheit. It rarely reaches 90 degrees at Index, and usually gets no hotter than 80 degrees. Afternoon thunderstorms are not uncommon in July and August.

On some cold winter days, Index may still be climbable, since the walls face south. On cold winter days, ice is sometimes in shape in Leavenworth, and even at Index if it's really cold!

STYLE AND ETHICS

While it has not been widely understood or recognized, there is a difference between style and ethics in rock climbing. Style is how you climb on the rock; ethics are what you do to the rock. Thus, hangdogging is a style; rappel bolting is an ethic (or lack of one).

Stylistic trends, such as hangdogging, rappel inspection, rehearsing, top-roping, pre-protection, free-soloing, et cetera, are relatively meaningless. It really makes no difference *how* you climb, so long as you aren't abusive to other climbers. While many styles are frowned upon by many (e.g., hangdogging, free-soloing), there are others who readily embrace them. As a basic rule, as long as you aren't trashing the rock or each other, go for it!

Ethical trends, such as bolting, chiseling holds, scarring cracks, and gardening are a bit more meaningful, and some are even disturbing. Gardening obviously has its place in Washington. Most new routes were once veritable gardens of ferns, moss, and bushes. Unearthing new routes is a tradition in Washington. Bolting, while "legitimate," has recently gotten out of control. With power drills in hand, many of Washington's current "pioneers" are bolting without restraint. Old, established aid lines are mercilessly bolted and pushed free; even established free climbs have had bolts added. Some restraint should be exercised in bolting; not every route needs to be bolted. Chiseling holds is absolutely not acceptable. If you need to chop a hold to climb the route, it is too hard for you. Let someone who is capable climb the route. Pitons have all but been abandoned except on difficult aid climbs. However, they have left their mark on many areas, most notably Index. Many of Index's hardest free climbs, including City Park, were made possible by years of direct aid placement and removal. However, as such piton routes go free, they should not be nailed. Still, many continue to nail free climbs, sometimes as a protest to the selfishness of free climbers who have very recently bolted several popular aid testpieces.

There is no last word on ethics and style. Styles and ethics come and go and change with the times. So, while rappel bolting is popular now, perhaps in ten years, after everything has been bolted, it will be considered a disgrace. Climbers should ask themselves whether they are doing any harm. If they feel that they are, then they should stop. Bolting, pitoning, and chopping holds are a dangerous legacy for us to leave to the future generations of climbers. Please be considerate and mindful of others whenever possible.

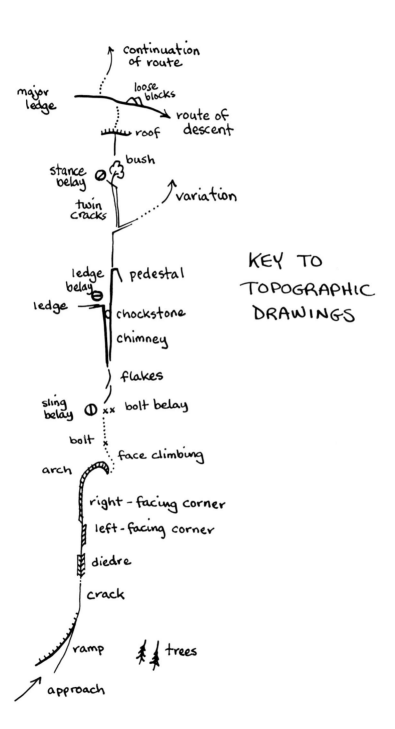

continuation
of route

major
ledge

loose
blocks

route of
descent

roof

bush

stance
belay

variation

twin
cracks

ledge
belay

pedestal

ledge

chockstone

chimney

flakes

sling
belay

bolt belay

bolt

face climbing

arch

right-facing corner

left-facing corner

diedre

crack

ramp

trees

approach

KEY TO
TOPOGRAPHIC
DRAWINGS

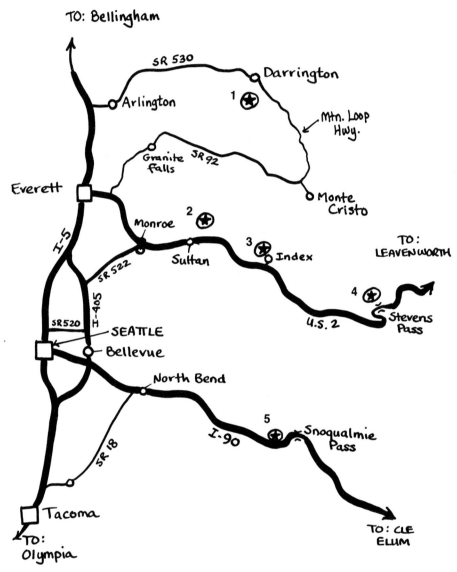

1. Darrington
2. Static Point
3. Index Town Walls
4. Ramone Rock
5. Fun Forest/Blondie Bluff

DARRINGTON

Darrington is one of the most underrated rock climbing areas in Washington, but by all accounts, it shouldn't be. It has excellent rock, interesting climbing, and is situated close enough to the Puget Sound sprawl to make it a popular area. Still, it goes begging for climbers. Perhaps it is the weather, the moss and dirt, or else the fact that Index has become the place to be (and be seen). When it comes right down to it, nobody goes to Darrington. (That's okay, though. There isn't enough parking.)

But somebody must, as there are several established routes on Darrington's slabby walls. Word has it that there are even a few new routes, although no one is willing to admit to having climbed them.

The town of Darrington is located 32 miles east of I-5 between Everett and Mt. Vernon, and is most quickly reached (from the west) by Highway 530. It is also possible to reach Darrington via the Mountain Loop Highway (unpaved) or by Highway 17A from Concrete.

To reach the climbing area, drive east through town, going straight where the main road bends left, and turn right at the coin-op laundry. The road is marked "To Mountain Loop Highway." Take a left on Sauk River Road. After three miles, turn right onto Road 2060 (unmarked) just before the Clear Creek Campground. The climbing areas are about five or six miles up the road. Apparently, as noted in a recent hiking guide, the forest service has recently renumbered all roads. Road 2060 was called Road 3210-A in *Washington Rock*.

Some words of caution about climbing at Darrington are in order. Many of the routes follow knobs and indistinct crack systems linked by blank slabs. Thus, routefinding may not be easy. Also, many routes feature long runouts with old ¼" bolts for protection — not a pleasant encounter for someone climbing at or near their limit. Generally, cruxes are well protected, but easier sections are usually not protected. Thus, on a 5.9 or 5.10, one can expect good protection at or near the crux, but not on the many 5.7 and 5.8 sections in between.

However, some "unprotected" sections may be protectable with small wired nuts. It is wise to carry a selection of small chocks on all routes, just in case. Take slings for rappel anchors, too.

It is wise to carry rain gear as well. Darrington is likely the wettest rock climbing area in Washington, if moss is a valid indicator.

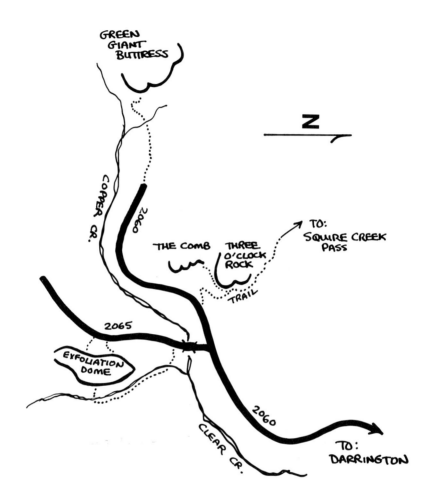

THREE O'CLOCK ROCK

About 5½ miles from the Mountain Loop Highway on Road 2060 (as identified by the marker at 5 miles) is the Squire Pass trailhead. By the time you get that far, you will need no description of Three O'Clock Rock nor of Comb Buttress; both will be plainly visible from the road. Hike for about 45 minutes up the trail to reach the toe of the rock. A steep scramble leads up to the **Big Tree** area. Continue higher up the trail to reach the North Buttress and Squire Creek Pass.

The **Big Tree/Kone** area is the most popular, both because it is the easiest to reach and because it has most of the best climbing at Darrington. Many parties rappel and climb their way across from **Big Tree** to **Tidbits**, climbing all the best pitches and, unfortunately, clogging up the routes.

The North Buttress has only four known routes, all long, slab or face climbs.

A crude trail traverses the base of the rock. Beyond **Tidbits**, the **Rash** and **Conan's Crack** provide good references for other routes. The trail continues upward to Comb Buttress.

THREE O'CLOCK ROCK

SOUTH BUTTRESS

1. **THE JINX** **5.9** (not shown)

    This route begins right of the Big Tree routes, at the divide between the north and south buttresses. A bolt marks the route. Climb to arching layback, then up and past roof. Rappel. Protection to 2". FA: Bob VanBelle, Doug White, Jeff Alington 1980.

2. **BIG TREE TWO** **II, 5.7 (R)**

    From the first belay on Big Tree One, climb obliquely right, over dihedrals, to tree. Continue up somewhat runout slabs. Two variations reach a pedestal. Traverse left to Big Tree. Protection to 3". FA: Jim Friar, Don Williamson 1970.

3. **BIG TREE ONE** **II, 5.7**

    This route begins near where the trail meets the rock, taking an obvious wide crack up a slab. Skirt roof on the right, then directly up corners (stay right), then left to reach the Big Tree. Descent described later. Protection to 3". FA: Manuel Gonzales, Don Williamson 1970. Variation: Dick's Demise 5.7 Climb left corner to the Big Tree. FA: Dick Bourgin, Van Brinkerhoff 1974.

North Buttress

South Buttress

Big Tree

10

9

6

5

4

3

2

1

THREE O' CLOCK ROCK

4. **CORNUCOPIA** ★ II, 5.9+
Left of the start of the **Big Tree** routes is a long, easy flake. Climb slab over roof to bolt belay, and continue up runout slab to meet **Dick's Demise**. Stay left to Big Tree. Rappel to the Kone and off. Protection to 3". FA: Don Brooks, Chris Syrjala 1980.

5. **THE QUIN KONEHEAD PRE-MEMORIAL ROUTE (THE KONE)** ★★★ II, 5.9
Left of Cornucopia is this slab route. The first pitch passes a small roof. Continue up easy slab pitch, then leftward to left edge of prominent roof. Final pitch to rappel. Protection to 1". FA: Duane Constantino, Dave Whitelaw 1978.

6. **TIDBITS** ★★★ II, 5.10b
Left of the start of the **Kone** about 200 feet, beyond the large roofs, a small dike (or 3rd class scrambing on right) leads to a belay. Continue up slabs, through a roof, to the "A" (an apex formed by facing dihedrals). Exit left, then right to the rappel anchors. Rappel the route. Protection to 1". FA: Duane Constantino, Dave Whitelaw, Tom Saunders, Rich Thompson 1978.

7. **GASTROBLAST** ★★ 5.10a
From the bottom of the "A" on **Tidbits**, strike out rightward on bolted slab to meet the **Kone** at its third belay. Fixed protection. FA: Dave Whitelaw and party.

8. **MAGIC BUS** II, 5.8
Left of **Tidbits**, where the trail slopes up, climb over a small roof. Continue for six pitches, bearing rightward, to finish above the Big Tree. Rappel to Big Tree. Protection to 3". FA: Peter Wojcik, Steve Risse, Mark McKillop 1979.

9. **WHEN BUTTERFLIES KISS BUMBLEBEES** 5.8
About 50 yards right of the start of **Shot in the Dark** is a flake system (left of two dihedrals). Climb this past roof to belay. Continue rightward, over dihedral, to knobby slab. Rappel route. Protection to 1". FA: Peter Wojcik, Mark McKillop 1979.

10. **RASHIONALIZATION** 5.7 (X)
Climb rightmost dihedral right of start of **Butterflies** to shared belay. Continue up the Rash (a knob-studded slab), then skirt left around blocks to belay. Rappel route. Protection to 3". FA: Don Brooks, Chris Syrjala 1980.

11. **LUKE 9:25** 5.10a (R) (not shown)
This recent addition begins as does **Shot in the Dark**. From the first bolt, go right to second bolt, then up to bolt belay. Second pitch follows bolted slab (knobs) to meet **Butterflies**. All bolts, but a small (#0) TCU recommended. FA: Tom Heins, Mike Altig 1988.

12. **SHOT IN THE DARK** ★ II, 5.10d (R)
About 100 yards left of **Tidbits** is a cluster of curved cedars. Climb a mossy arch to runout slab. Continue up through two roofs. The crux is at the end of the third pitch. Rappel the route. Protection to 3". FA: Duane Constantino, Marv Wetzel, Steve Scott 1978.

13. **CONAN'S CRACK** II, 5.8
The obvious right-facing dihedral on the far left side. Climb four pitches, then rappel. Protection to 6". FA: Don Brooks, Brent Hoffman 1973.

14. **THE PLAN** II, 5.8 (not shown)
From the first belay on **Conan**, climb short crack on left, continuing up two more pitches into the trees. Rappel. Protection to 2". FA: Lou Dangles, Clark Gerdhart 1973.

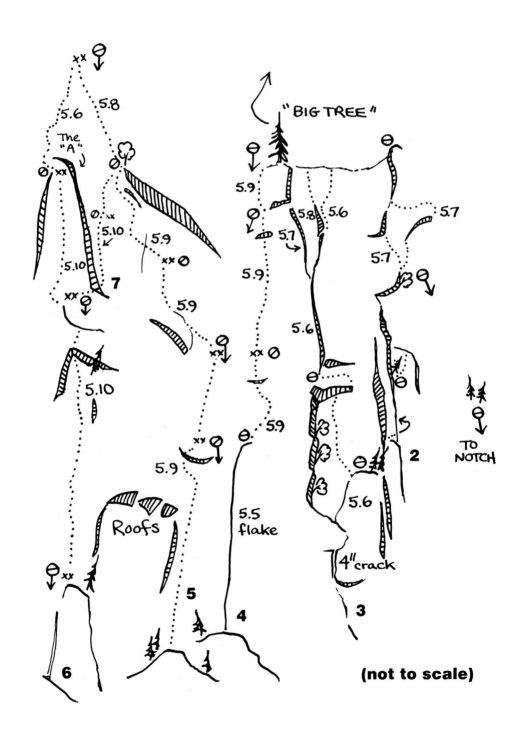

THREE O' CLOCK ROCK – SOUTH BUTTRESS

THREE O' CLOCK ROCK – SOUTH BUTTRESS

15. **SHRIMPSIDE   5.7**   (not shown)
Left of Conan is the "Frosted Flake". Scrambling and Class 5 climbing reach the flake. Rappel from the flake's top. Protection to ½". FA: Don Brooks, Dave Shrimpton 1980.
16. **URBAN PLOUGHBOY   5.8**   (not shown)
A left-facing dihedral 50 feet left of Shrimpside. Rappel the route. Protection to 3"; take several large pieces. FA: Don Brooks 1980.
17. **TRUNKLINE   5.9**   (not shown)
Traverse right from below the Frosted Flake to an off-width on the right. Protection to 4". FA: Don Brooks, Dave Shrimpton 1980.

NORTH BUTTRESS

The following routes are found on the broad slab of the North Buttress, right of the gully where the Jinx begins.

18. **RUBBER SOUL** ★ **II, 5.8 (R)**

On the north buttress, far right of the Big Tree routes, is this six-pitch route which climbs an obvious white dike. Begin with long, traversing pitch and a roof to reach the dike. Rappel the Bushy Galore route. Protection to 1½". FA: Don Brooks, Don Harder, Donn Heller 1973.

19. **BUSHY GALORE** **III, 5.7**

Climb the large, grassy dihedral right of Rubber Soul for as many as 10 pitches. It is possible to rappel after five pitches. Protection to 2". FA: Dave Davis, Donn Heller, 1972.

20. **SILENT RUNNING** ★★ **II, 5.9 (R)**

Right of Bushy Galore is this four-pitch slab route, starting with a small roof about 100 feet off the ground. Stray right to bolted slab, then straight up. Can rappel after two pitches. Protection to 2". FA: Don Brooks, Brent Hoffman 1973.

21. **BEANBERRY DELIGHT** **II, 5.8 (R)**

Right of Silent Running is a ledge with two cedars. Two scrambling approaches, either from the right (Class 4) or direct (Class 3 and 4), reach the ledge. Climb straight above ledge to fourth bolt on second pitch of Silent Running, then swing right around roof; cross Silent Running, up to belay, then across Silent Running again to corner. Continue up corner to rappel route. Protection to 1". FA: Don Brooks, Dennis Fenstermaker, Brent Hoffman 1973. Variation: Connect first tree belay of Beanberry with first belay of Silent Running (5.9). Long runout. Protection to 2". FA: unknown.

THE COMB

The Comb, or Comb Buttress, is the large, multi-buttressed slab immediately left of and above Three O'Clock Rock. The buttresses stand out as clean rock surrounded by dark, forested slabs and gullies.

From near Magic Bus, take a crude trail leftward to reach the rightmost slabs of the Comb.

Despite the obvious potential of this cliff, few routes have been done here. There is potential for several three to five pitch routes.

1. **SKY RIDER** ★ **II, 5.10a**

On the second "tooth" of the Comb, left and downhill from where the path reaches the cliff, climb a gully, then traverse right to a grassy crack. Continue over wide roof crack, the right around (or over) second roof. Rappel from a large tree. Protection to 3". FA: Chris Greyell, Duane Constantino 1979.

2. **BARRINGTON'S REVENGE** **5.7** (not shown)

A short crack right of the start of Sky Rider. Downclimb left. Protection to 1½". FA: Dave Anderson, Don Brooks, Donn Heller 1974.

3. **BUMP CITY** **5.8**

From the base of the crag, this is visible as a steep, knobby wall. Begin left of a white dike below a short, horizontal crack. Two pitches. Protection to 1". FA: Don Brooks, Donn Heller 1974.

COMB BUTTRESS

GREEN GIANT BUTTRESS

Hidden at the head of Copper Creek Valley is Green Giant Buttress, which surely ranks as one of Washington's finest rock climbing cliffs, except for the horrendous approach.

Drive to the end of Road 2060 (or as close as you can get without losing your transmission), then hike towards the wall. The trail, while fairly obvious, can be missed. Generally, stay straight into the woods, rather than up or down on the newest logging cuts. The trail crosses a boulder field to reach a blocky creekbed, then turns right up a dry creekbed, through brush, to a gravel wash which reaches the base of the wall. See the map for best results, and good luck!

The routes are easy to locate. Avoidance climbs the most obvious left-hand gully/ dihedral system, while Botany 101 takes the huge gully/dihedral left of the formidable prow of the buttress. Dreamer climbs the buttress left of Botany 101, while the Fast Lane takes the prominent prow on the right.

Descents are made by rappel, Avoidance from the left, all others from the right. From Botany 101's finish, head down a gully until you need to rappel. Some can make do with only two rappels, while others use five. If in doubt, rappel.

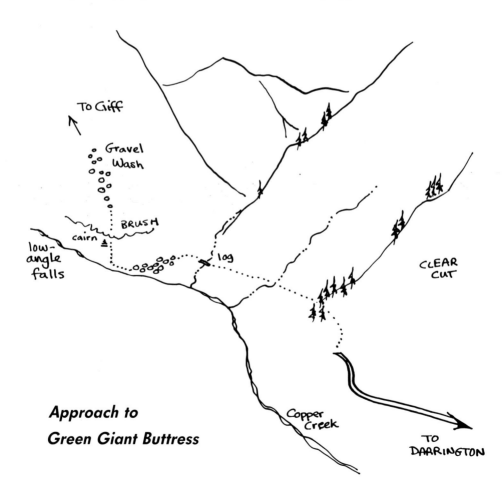

Approach to

Green Giant Buttress

GREEN GIANT BUTTRESS

GREEN GIANT BUTTRESS ROUTES

1. **AVOIDANCE** **III, 5.8**
   The obvious gully/chimney on the left flank of the wall. Exit chimney on left near top. Rappel left to brushy descent. Protection to 2″. FA: Don Brooks, Mark White 1972.

2. **TAKE THE RUNOUT** **II, 5.10 (R/X)**
   From where Avoidance begins, climb obliquely rightward. Traverse right with poor or no protection, then jump into a bush, or some such nonsense. Meets Dreamer at second belay. Protection to 1½″. FA: Duane Constantino, Chris Greyell 1979.

3. **GIANT'S TEARS** **II, 5.10d A0**
   From first belay of Runout, climb bolted slab (aid moves), then up cracks and corners to meet Dreamer at fourth belay. Aid can be eliminated by staying left on Runout to bypass bolted slab. Protection to 2″. FA: Duane Constantino (and partner?).

4. **DREAMER** ★★★ **IV, 5.9**
   From base of Botany 101 dihedral, stray left up cracks and slabs. Continue up more of the same. Ten pitches. Protection to 3″. FA: Duane Constantino, Chris Greyell 1979.

5. **BOTANY 101** **III, 5.8**
   Obvious, slanting dihedral. Up to 10 pitches. Protection to 3″. FA: Don Brooks, Brent Hoffman 1975.

6. **LOST IN SPACE** **II, 5.10a**
   After three pitches of Botany 101, strike rightward up flakes to crux finger crack. Meets Fast Lane. Protection to 2″. FA: Duane Constantino, Wally Barker.

7. **THE FAST LANE** ★★ **5.11b/c (PG-13/R)**
   From near Botany's start, climb bolted face rightward, and continue up cracks and face to pedestal. Face climb up the "Greyellian Rib," then move left to cracks left of crest. Move right around Great Roof and up face, crossing rib again. Crux pitch leads over roof to thin, dirty cracks. Two easy pitches lead to the top. Protection to 2″; camming units. May be a bit dirty for free climbing. FA: Duane Constantino, Chris Greyell 1979; FFA: Andy Cairns, Brian Burdo 1986.

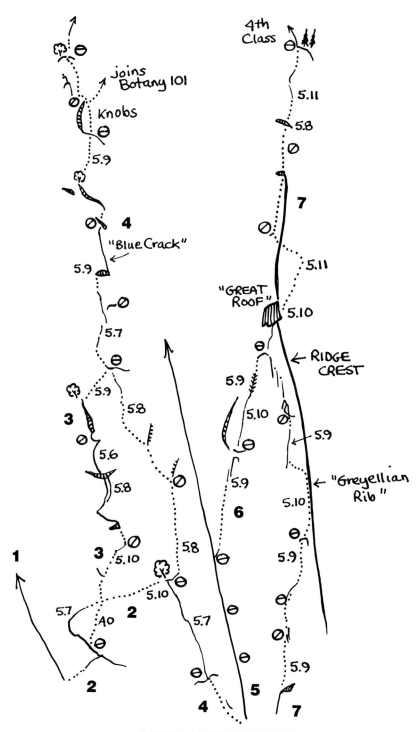

GREEN GIANT BUTTRESS

EXFOLIATION DOME

Exfoliation Dome is the massive rock spur of Helena Peak located almost directly south of the fork where Road 2065 splits off from 2060. The dome is an "isolated peak" according to Fred Beckey's 1976 guide, and is the most arduous and serious climbing objective in Darrington. As with Waterfall Column and Jupiter Rock in Leavenworth, ascents of Exfoliation have complex, long approaches, multi-pitch, serious routes, and difficult descents. More than one party has been caught on the dome after dark. Wisely, most stayed put until morning. Be prepared to wait out bad weather or darkness, as it would be foolish to attempt to descend the dome in either condition, especially darkness.

To approach the eastern, or "Witch Doctor" wall, drive up Road 2065 (the left fork) about ½ mile beyond the fork, and park at an old logging spur "road" on the left. Follow the creekbed, staying right at junctions, to where you can reach the wall. Plan on more than one hour for the approach.

The western slabs, or Blueberry Hill, are as time consuming to approach, but more direct. Drive up Road 2065 about one mile to the "Granite Sidewalk." Hike up the slabs to the base of the cliff. This is not a good approach to try in wet weather, as the low-angle slabs can become very slippery.

Descents range from merely unpleasant to downright dangerous. Numerous descents have been pioneered, although two are considered "standard." The most commonly used descent is the **West Slab** rappel route. However, this descent is unpleasant. Better is the 23rd Psalm rappel, down the route. This descent is hard to find from above, but once located offers 10 straightforward rappels down to the Granite Sidewalk. The North Ridge and the "woods" north of 23rd Psalm have been rappelled, but are decidedly unpleasant and time consuming. During bad weather, the quickest descent is via the southeast buttress, on the Witch Doctor Wall side. Three rappels lead to the trees. However, once down, a long walk awaits you. Therefore, this descent is best used only when a quick way off the dome is needed.

Be aware that rock on Blueberry Hill is "active," in that large rockfalls have and continue to occur. Of course, the same has occurred at Index, but in neither case are the rockfalls regular occurrences. Just be aware that they do occur. Be careful of new rock scars — surrounding rock is probably still loose.

BLUEBERRY HILL

The "back" side of Exfoliation Dome is this broad slab. The vividly exfoliated rock is straffed with odd corners, roofs and ledges. It would appear that many routes could be pioneered here.

Beware of rockfall, and bad weather. Descents are described in the introduction to Exfoliation Dome.

1. **NORTH RIDGE   II, 5.7 A1**
   Three belayed pitches, some scrambling on or near crest of ridge. Protection to 1"; some thin pitons. FA: Greg Ball, Bill Fryberger 1973.

2. **UNKNOWN   5.10 A3(?)**
   An unknown route which is believed to take the steep buttress shown in the photo. However, it may not be anywhere near this, so if you climb this line and don't find a "route," please let the publisher know. Also, beware of loose rock, as some large flakes have recently peeled off. FA: unknown.

3. **TWENTY-THIRD PSALM   IV, 5.8 A3+**
   Nuts and pitons to 2½"; 25 pieces, including rurps, bathooks. Questionable rock on third pitch, due to "recent" rockfall. Five pitches of aid; five free. FA: Dave Whitelaw, Chris Greyell 1978.

4. **WEST BUTTRESS (aka BLUEBERRY HILL)   III, 5.8**
   Stroll up the Granite Sidewalk to left side of right-facing corner system. Moderate climbing. Protection to 2". FA: Clark Gerhardt, Bill Sumner 1972.

5. **WEST SLAB   III, 5.8**
   At the top of the Granite Sidewalk, climb slabs just right of West Buttress directly to ridge crest. Protection to 3". FA: Manuel Gonzales, Tom Oas 1970.

BLUEBERRY HILL

WITCH DOCTOR WALL

The Witch Doctor Wall is the most dramatic of Darrington's walls, and one of the most difficult to approach, its only rival in that respect being Green Giant Buttress.

There are six routes, mostly involving multiple aid pitches. Descents are described in the previous section.

As with any other "big wall," be prepared for anything, including bad weather and bivouacking.

1. **ORANGE BLOSSOM SPECIAL** (−★) **II, 5.9** (not shown)
   This route takes the massively obvious chimney on the far left side of the wall. There is some 5.8 chimneying until the chimney becomes too wide; then stay on the right. Protection to 4" (?); take 165-foot rope. FA: Sprague Ackley, Hope Barnes 1982.

2. **WITCH DOCTOR'S ELIXIR** (−★) **III, 5.9** (not shown)
   About 500 feet right (north) of Orange Blossom Special, start at the highest fir on the base of the wall left of the Witch Doctor route. Largely unknown. Dirty. FA: Sprague Ackley, Hope Barnes 1982.

3. **THE WITCH DOCTOR   V, 5.7 A3**
   Nuts and pins to 2½"; 40 pieces, including KBs. FA: Fred Beckey, David Wagner, Tom Nephew 1969.

4. **SUNDAY CRUISE   III, 5.9**
   From Great Arch on Checkered Demon, traverse left into long dihedral/crack system. Protection to 3"; many small. FA: Dave Tower, Duane Constantino, Chris Greyell 1979.

5. **THE CHECKERED DEMON   V, 5.7 A3**
   The very obvious arch. Nuts and pitons to 3"; 50 pieces, including rurp and many LAs. FA: Dave Davis, Don Leonard, Bill Lingley 1971.

6. **THUNDER ROAD   IV, 5.6 A3**
   Nuts and pitons to 1½"; mostly pitons, including many LAs. FA: Don Brooks (solo).

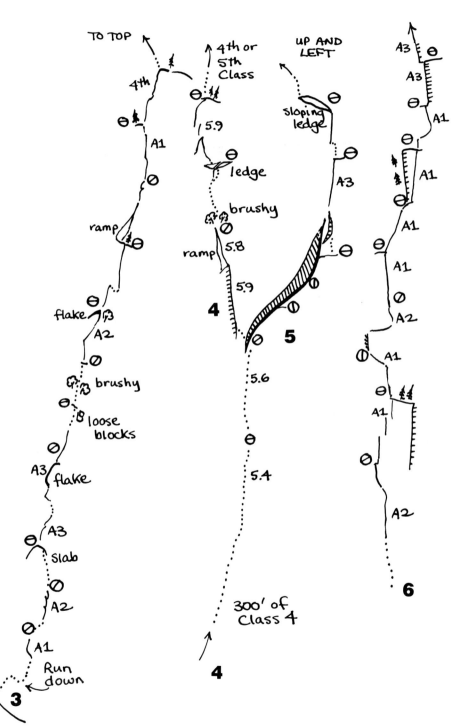

WITCH DOCTOR WALL

STATIC POINT

Static Point is a large, slabby granite buttress stuck way out in the woods north of Sultan, so remote that it was "discovered" by airplane. Logging road access made it possible to drive to within about an hour's walk of the cliff; however, new logging activity has shortened the walk (in addition to worsening the ambience of the area with typical rampant clear cutting). Impending logging threatens to shorten the hike even more, making it very possible that Static Point will soon become a "sport crag."

The routes on Static Point rarely vary. Mostly they involve moderately angled slab climbing on moderately smooth granite with widely spaced protection, usually in the form of ¼" bolts (according to some reports, a few of these bolts can be pulled out by hand!). It is not uncommon to go 30 or 40 feet between bolts. Thus, these routes are fairly serious, although in the same sense as Glacier Point Apron (Yosemite) routes, since, as the cliff is rarely too steep, falls are most often long sliders. However, if a bolt pulls out, forget it! Be aware that, as most of the routes involve continuous friction on somewhat smooth granite, "sticky" shoes are recommended.

Because most of the routes involve several pitches of climbing at an area miles distant from anything, committment is a factor for climbers to consider. The weather is typically similar to the weather at Index, although in many ways it is said to resemble Leavenworth. Southern exposure generally guarantees faster drying time, but good luck picking a non-rainy day. In the spring, however, snow lingers longer and temperatures are generally cooler.

It is difficult to judge the angle and direction of routes using the topos in this guide (or any guide). Routes that appear to go one direction on topos actually finish above routes which appear to go another direction. Remember that Static Point is not flat, but curved, and dome-like. Thus, a route beginning on the left may finish at the same place as one on the right side.

Driving to Static Point is time consuming, though not too difficult. Just east of Sultan, turn north onto Olney Road (just west of the saw shop, the road is marked "Sultan Basin Recreation Area"). Follow this road (stay left where the road forks) for about 18 miles, to very near Spada Reservoir. A new logging spur (the second on the right at this point) is taken to where it is difficult (or impossible) to continue by car. Walk from here. The approach hike leaves this road at the obvious lefthand gully/drainage, and reaches Static Point's left side.

Visitors to this area may wish to consult David Whitelaw's trendy *Private Dancer* (Tundra Press, 1985) for further information (and unusual graphics). Overall, however, this guide should suffice.

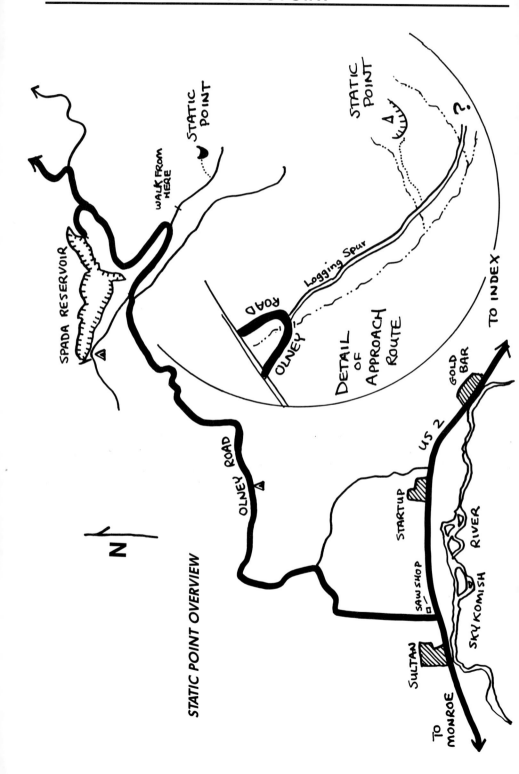

STATIC POINT OVERVIEW

N

SPADA RESERVOIR

WALK FROM HERE

STATIC POINT

OLNEY ROAD

OLNEY ROAD

Logging Spur

STATIC POINT

DETAIL OF APPROACH ROUTE

TO INDEX

GOLD BAR

US 2

STARTUP

SAW SHOP

SKYKOMISH RIVER

SULTAN

TO MONROE

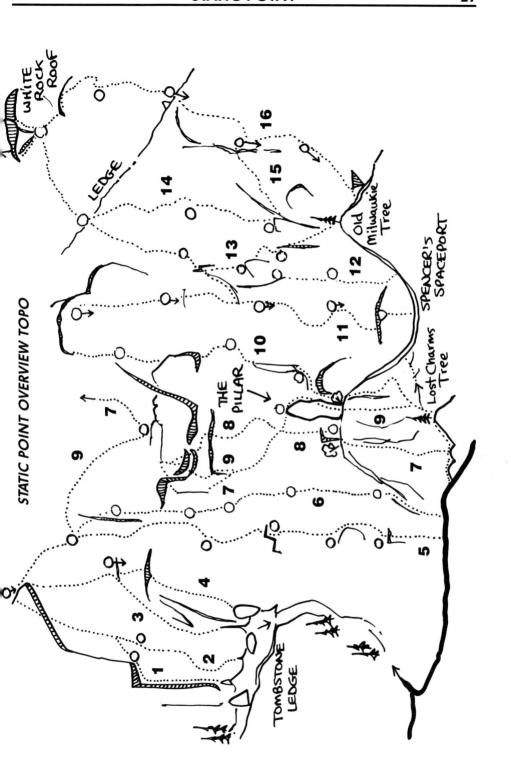

STATIC POINT OVERVIEW TOPO

WHITE ROCK ROOF

LEDGE

Old Milwaukie Tree

SPEAKER'S SPACEPORT

Lost Charms Tree

THE PILLAR

TOMBSTONE LEDGE

TOMBSTONE LEDGE

Tombstone Ledge is perhaps the most obvious feature of Static Point. Situated on the far left, this terrace is named for a large block of granite perched at the left side of the ledge. Four routes begin here, and several others may reach the ledge during the descent. Tombstone Ledge may be reached most easily via a third-class scramble.

1. **THE CORNER   5.8**
   On the left side of Tombstone Ledge, right of the Tombstone, climb an obvious right-facing dihedral (obvious because it is the only one in the area). The second pitch climbs to join **Cashman** on the easy slab right of the dihedral/arch, with a healthy runout. Protection to 3″. FA: Duane Constantino, Dave Whitelaw 1983.

2. **CASHMAN   ★★ 5.10c (R/X)**
   Just right of **The Corner**, begin in a shallow corner and climb unprotected hard moves left to a solution pocket and the first bolt. From there, more unprotected climbing leads back rightward to more bolts and, just above a small roof, the belay. Continue upward to single bolt, then long easy runout to **Black Fly**. Bolts. FA: Dave Whitelaw, Bob DeChenne 1983.

3. **BLACK FLY   5.8 (R/X)**
   Begin in a shallow corner right of **Cashman**, and left of the rotten pillar start of **American Pie**. Climb the corner and flakes to reach the bolts. Somewhat unprotected climbing leads upwards and right to the belay. An easy but entirely unprotected pitch leads to another belay. Rappel back to the ledge. Protection to ½″, with small wireds. FA: Chris Greyell, Dave Whitelaw 1983.

4. **AMERICAN PIE   ★★★ 5.10a (R)**
   An excellent pitch leads from the rotten pillar at the right end of Tombstone Ledge, through a roof, to meet **Black Fly**. The crux comes just before the belay, well out from the last bolt. It is said to be easier to stay a bit left. Bolts, #2½ Friend. FA: Dave Whitelaw, Duane Constantino 1983.

5. **ON LINE   ★★★ 5.10b (R)**
   This direct Static Point classic begins some distance right of the third-class approach to Tombstone Ledge. Look for the first bolt (40 feet up), and a short corner/roof. For the remainder of the route's six pitches, bolts predominately dictate the line. There are some sporting runouts. A long rope is recommended (the first pitch is 170 feet long). Bolts, but include a #1½ Friend. FA: Don Brooks, Dave Whitelaw 1983.

6. **OFF LINE   II, 5.10a (R)**
   About 40 feet right of the start of **On Line** is a recent route, which parallels **On Line** for five pitches before joining that route at its fifth belay. Begin by climbing past dihedrals for two pitches, then up slab through overlaps. The fifth pitch is more direct, following bolts. Protection to 1″, with many small wireds. FA: Unknown.

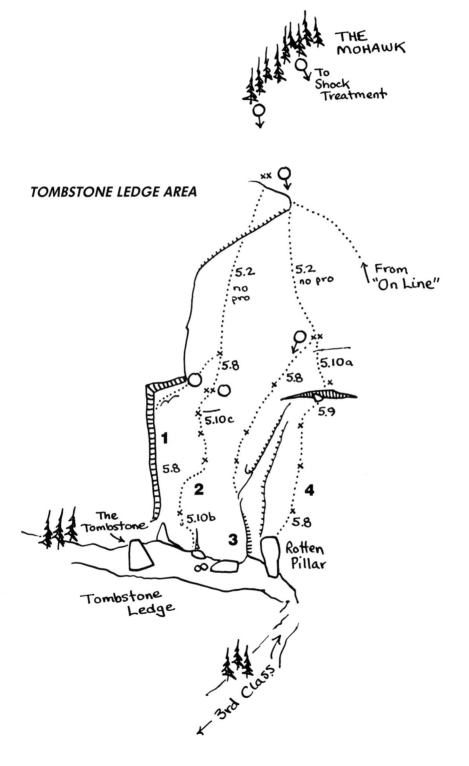

THE MOHAWK

To Shock Treatment

TOMBSTONE LEDGE AREA

xx

5.2 no pro

5.2 no pro

↑ From "On Line"

xx

5.10a

5.8

5.8

5.9

5.8

5.10c

1

5.8

2

5.10b

The Tombstone

4

5.8

3

Rotten Pillar

Tombstone Ledge

3rd Class

THE PILLAR AREA

Some distance right of Tombstone Ledge is "The Pillar," a 130-foot-high detached rock situated some two pitches up, directly above the "Lost Charms Tree." Routes in this area tend to follow natural features of the rock, and thus have fewer bolts. Above the Pillar, the routes pass a prominent roof band. Above that, it is possible to exit via two possible routes, which are discussed in the text.

It shoud be noted that approaching along the "base" of the cliff is somewhat complicated here. The true base of the slab drops off just beyond Off Line. To stay with the routes, traverse straight across the exfoliations (some exposure, possibly fifth-class moves).

7. **McCARTHY/CARLSTAD   II, 5.9**
   Begin downhill and left from the Lost Charms Tree (about 200 feet right of On Line) at a tree atop a pedestal. Climb two pitches to the Pillar, then up the left side of the Pillar to join the Pillar route for one pitch. From the fourth belay, stay left to a crack and roof to rejoin The Pillar route. The original party climbed an easy righthand flake to the trees; most parties go left across the "Fluourescent Green Crab Traverse" (?), which makes the route 5.10c. Protection to 3". FA: Jim McCarthy, Rich Carlstad 1983.

8. **OLD WEIRD HAROLD   5.10a (R/X)**
   From the Pillar Ledge, beginning just left of the Pillar, climb two pitches direcly left of and above the Pillar, through the roofs, to rejoin The Pillar route higher up. Long runouts. Protection to 3". FA: Dave Whitelaw, John Downing 1984.

9. **THE PILLAR   II, 5.10c (R)**
   This route shares the first 30 feet of Lost Charms, then strikes left (straight up) to the base of the Pillar. Climb the Pillar face until forced onto the right side. From the Pillar's top, wander leftward to belay left of a long, thin roof. Turn the roof at its left terminus, and pass higher roofs to reach a grassy crack and ledge. The left exit and "Fluorescent Green Crab Traverse" are the proper finish for this route. Protection to 3". FA: Chris Greyell, Duane Constantino, Dave Whitelaw, January 1984.

10. **LOST CHARMS   II, 5.10b**
    From the "Lost Charms Tree," climb up and rightward, then back left into corner system to the Pillar Ledge. Climb up just right of the Pillar, then cross the aptly named "Bridge Flake" and belay at its far side. Continue up a finger crack to ledges, then left up flakes to the "Great Flake." From there, it is possible to head left to reach the "Mohawk," from where it is possible to rappel to Tombstone Ledge. However, a direct finish was recently added. From the top of the Great Flake, climb directly up the slab to reach the left side of a prominent arch. Traverse the arch to the Shock Treatment rappel. Protection to 3". FA: Chris Greyell, Bob DeChenne, Pete Skardtvedt 1983; Direct Finish: Chris Greyell, Dave Whitelaw 1986.

SPENCER'S SPACEPORT

Right of the Lost Charms Tree, and up half a pitch, is this curiously named ledge system, from which Shock Treatment and The Curious Cube begin (along with Static Cling and Fuddhat). The easiest way to reach the Spaceport is to traverse a ledge rightward from the first pitch of Lost Charms. Many parties do not rope up for the "scramble" to the Spaceport, but it is recommended here because there is some moderate fifth-class climbing to be encountered. At the far, upper right end of the ledge is the "Old Milwaukie Tree."

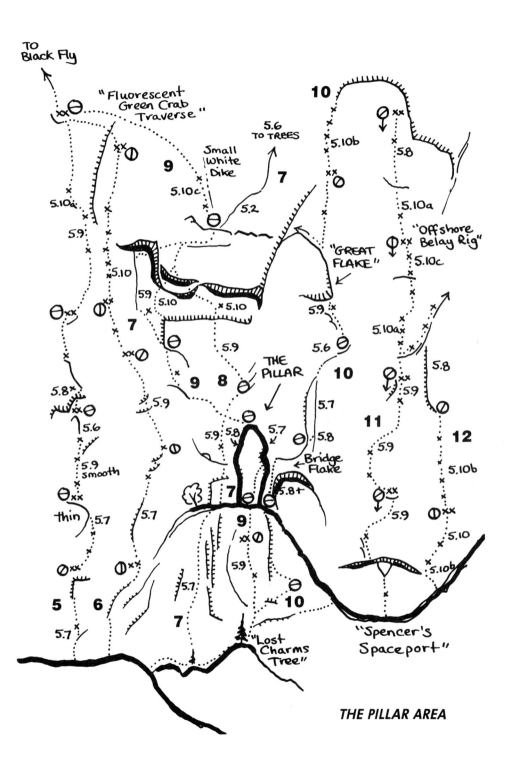

THE PILLAR AREA

11. **SHOCK TREATMENT**   ★★★ III, 5.10c (R)

One of the most popular routes at Static Point, this begins at the lowest point of the Spaceport. Climb past a bolt to a roof, then up unprotected slabs (one bolt on left) to stance. Continue left and up past bolts to flakes. The third pitch climbs past several bolts, with two distinct cruxes; this pitch finishes at a sling belay known as the "Offshore Belay Rig." A final pitch leads to the "Broken Band." Rappel the route. Numerous long runouts. Protection to 3". FA: Chris Greyell, Dave Tower, Dave Whitelaw 1984. Note: It is possible to avoid the crux pitch by traversing right up ramps to join The Curious Cube on that route's third pitch.

12. **ARTIE RIP**   ★ II, 5.10b (R)

Right of the start of Shock Treatment is this three-pitch addition, which connects with the variation traverse mentioned above. The first pitch begins just right of the low roof, climbs to the roof's right margin, then climbs a sparsely bolted slab. There is some runout 5.10 climbing here. The second pitch is more bolted slab, which reaches the final corner and eventually connects with the Cube. Protection to 1½". FA: Dave Whitelaw, Chris Greyell 1986.

13. **THE CURIOUS CUBE**   III, 5.9+ (R)

This is the original Static Point route. Begin from the Old Milwaukie Tree and climb leftward to a corner. Continue up right, then left to pillar/flake belay. Unprotected friction leads through a short dihedral/roof. The fourth pitch climbs past a flake, then runs it out up a knobby slab to reach the big ledge system. Fourth class rubble (loose) and some fifth class leads right and up to belay beneath a jumbo roof ("White Rock Roof"), where a hidden crack on the left leads to the Cube. Descent from the Cube is down a left-facing ramp to reach the Mohawk, then rappel to Shock Treatment and off. Protection to 3". FA: Buckley, Johnson, Pickard (?) 1983.

14. **STATIC CLING**   ★ II, 5.10a (R)

From the Old Milwaukie Tree, climb directly up a dihedral to a pedestal belay. Continue straight up poorly protected friction to a small overlap, and a short crux to a ledge. Climb a lefthand arch to more sparsely protected friction. May rappel route from third belay (which is the fourth belay of the Curious Cube). Bolts, but take RPs. FA: Dave Whitelaw, Chris Greyell 1984.

15. **THE NOD**   5.9

A variation of Static Cling which reaches Fuddhat's second belay. From the first belay of Static Cling, strike out rightward up face, following far-apart bolts. Protection includes #2 and #3 Friend. FA: Dave Whitelaw, S. Scott 1984.

16. **FUDDHAT**   ★★ III, 5.11c A0 (R)

Just down and right of the Old Milwaukie Tree, and just left of a triangular roof, climb up past a flake to bolts, then run it out to the belay. Continue rightward past flake to friction, and second belay. Traverse rightward to more friction, with a few more bolts, eventually reaching a large ledge system. It is possible to rappel down the route from here. Three additional pitches have been added, making it possible to reach the Cube. Continue up bolted slab, then traverse right (tension) to crack. Pass long, thin roof on the left to reach the fifth belay of The Curious Cube. Climb a short arch (crux, one point of aid) to the roof, then up and over. Protection to 3". FA: Dave Whitelaw, Chris Greyell 1984; Complete: Chris Greyell, Dave Whitelaw, Dave Jay 1987.

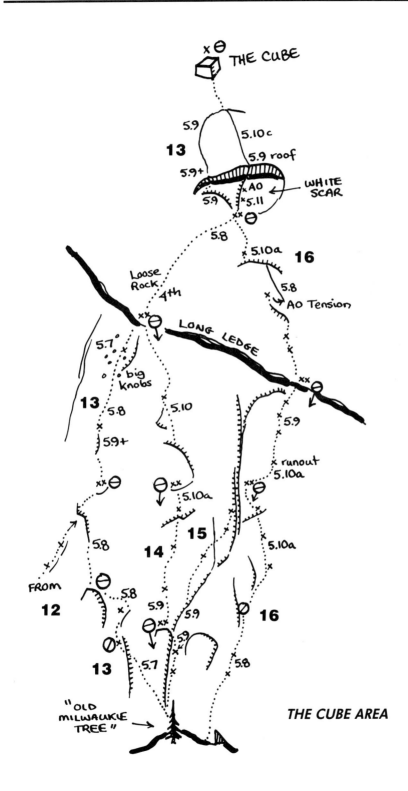

THE CUBE

5.9
5.10c
13
5.9 roof
5.9+
AO
5.11
WHITE SCAR
5.9
5.8
5.10a **16**
Loose Rock
5.8
AO Tension
4th
LONG LEDGE
5.7
big knobs
13
5.8
5.10
5.9
5.9+
runout 5.10a
5.10a
5.10a
15
14
5.8
5.10a
FROM
12
5.8
5.8
5.9
5.9
5.9
16
13
5.7
5.8
"OLD MILWAUKIE TREE"

THE CUBE AREA

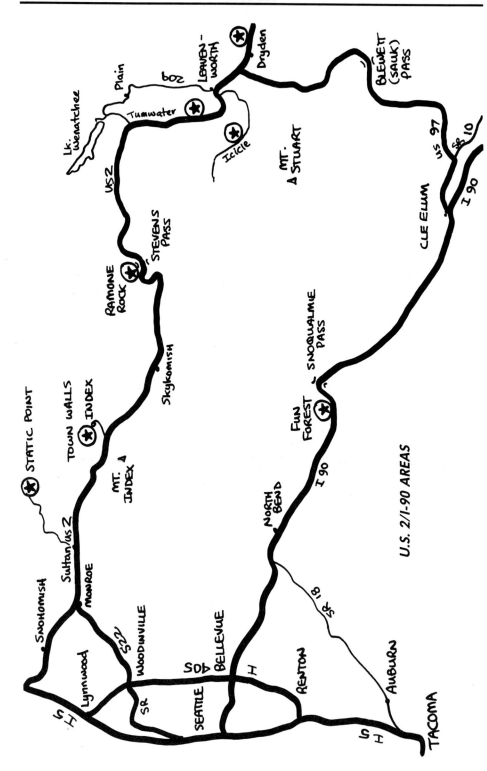

U.S. 2/I-90 AREAS

INDEX

The Index Town Walls, located about 40 miles east of Everett just off U.S. Highway 2, are becoming this state's most popular climbing area. The area is composed of two major cliffs – the Upper and Lower Town Walls – and countless smaller walls, crags and buttress hidden in the dense second (third, fourth?) growth alder, maple and fir forests above the small town of Index, Washington.

The industrial past of Index is well evidenced by the scars of turn of the century quarrying operations, which served to remove nearly half of the Lower Wall before the quarrying operations were halted. Granite removed from the area may be seen in building foundations throughout the northwest, including the Capitol steps in Olympia. Luckily, some rock was spared the drills and dynamite; what remains contains some of the finest granite climbing in this country.

The climbing at Index is decidedly steep, and up until the beginning of this decade, aid climbing was the predominate method of ascent. New attitudes about cleaning and protecting, combined with a learned intuition about what is possible, have driven local pioneers to free climb nearly every aid route on the Lower Wall. The legacy of aid is partly responsible for the freeing of most routes; pin scars left by countless aid ascents have served the new age of free climbers well.

The Lower Wall has some of the most difficult free routes in the state, including at least one 5.13 and many 5.12s and 5.11s. Most of the routes on the Lower Wall proper climb steep, thin cracks, while the upper half of the cliff is decidedly slabby. A narrow ledge system (the Park Bench) bisects the wall at mid-height. The left edge of the Lower Wall, the Great Northern Slab, has some of the easier routes in the area, as well as a few very difficult slab climbs.

Incidental cliffs near the Lower Wall include the Dihedral Wall, perched directly above Roger's Corner; The Country, a continuation of the original wall on the far right side of the cliff, past the immense quarry scar; the Garden Wall, a small wall on the lower left side of the cliff; the Lower Lump, a large wart of heavily fractured rock on the extreme left side; and the Inner Wall, a secluded canyon between the Lower Wall and Lower Lump.

The Upper Wall is still aid country, with numerous multi-pitch, difficult nailing extravaganzas; however, most of these routes now have free pitches mixed in, and are in danger of going all free after suitable scrubbing and/or bolting. There is a plethora of short, difficult free climbs along and near the base of the Upper Wall. The main cliff is so obvious from town that it needs no real description. The Upper Wall is divided into three distinct sections. The left side is a formidable, steep wall; the right side (The Cheeks) is split by a prominent ledge (Prance Platform) and a deep vertical gully; and The Diamond, a large face on the far right side, which is separated from the main formation by a wide gully. A trail passes along the base of the entire cliff.

Of the incidental cliffs near the Upper Wall, the largest is the Lookout Point formation, a forested "dome" located right of and below the Diamond. Below this is Private Idaho, a short cliff with several crack climbs. Directly below The Cheeks is Rattletale Wall, with a prominent dihedral. There are also a few small, unnamed cliffs hidden in the trees along the base of the wall, with routes that will be described in the text.

The text in this section will not follow an absolute left-to-right format. Instead, because the two main cliffs are the focal points of the climbing area, they will each have their own section. Satellite cliffs will follow. While at first the order of areas listed in this section may seem random, once you have climbed at Index, you will understand why they are ordered the way they are. You will likely spend most of your first days at Index climbing on the Lower Wall, possibly venturing to the Upper Wall. Later on, you will begin to explore the smaller, harder-to-reach crags. Thus, hopefully this arrangement will make sense to the readers.

The town of Index offers a few sparse amenities. There is a tavern, a store, and a restaurant/inn. However, there are few nearby campgrounds, no public showers, and very little in the way of entertainment. Most visiting climbers rough it near the river, or else drive over from Leavenworth or Seattle each day.

The weather at Index is much wetter than at Leavenworth, due to the convergence of wet, moist air with the colder, higher elevations of the Cascade Range. The clouds seem to get squeezed like a big sponge, then drift harmlessly over the mountains to dissipate in the heat of eastern Washington's sun. Thus, Index and Darrington get soaked, while Leavenworth stays at least partially dry. It is a good idea, even on a "sunny" day, to bring rain gear, at least in the spring and the fall. From late June to early September, the weather can usually be relied upon; at any other time, if it isn't raining, be thankful.

Since many long-established aid routes have now been climbed free, in whole or in part, it is important to limit hammered placements in these routes either for aid or free protection. Continued pitoning will further disfigure the rock, changing the character of these climbs for future aid and free ascents. Even on those routes which still require hammered placements, nailing can and should be kept to a necessary minimum. Routes such as **Ten-Percent** and **Snow White** have been done with almost no hammered placements. By all means, feel free to aid climb on routes which have been climbed free, but please climb them hammerless. For those desiring to learn pitoncraft, there are still a number of routes upon which one can hammer away, especially on the Upper Wall. However, use discretion, as many "aid" cracks are now free climbs. When in doubt, ask.

One final note: there are numerous bolts on Index's walls that were placed more than 20 years ago. Many of these bolts are suspect at best, and have been known to break. Efforts to replace bolts have been made on free climbs, but many aid climbs — especially on the Upper Wall — have ladders of rusty old bolts. If in doubt, back them up, or, where necessary, replace them.

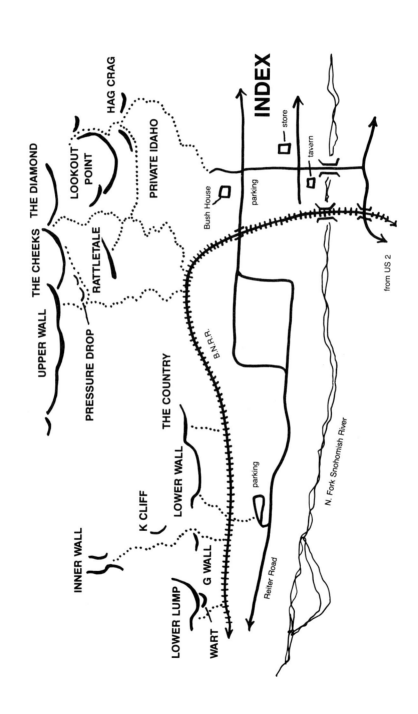

LOWER TOWN WALL

The Lower Town Wall surely ranks as one of Washington's finest crags, with perhaps the greatest concentration of steep cracks of any cliff in Washington. The cliff is located left of and below the Upper Wall, and is identifiable from town by a large white scar. The wall may be reached by driving southwest from town (take a left at the Bush House) along the narrow county road to a graded parking lot below the railroad tracks.

The lower wall is divided into several distinct sections. The slabby area on the left side is the Great Northern Slab ("The Slab"), which is flanked on the left by a dark, rotten wall, and on the right by Roger's Corner, a large dihedral. Directly above Roger's Corner is the Dihedral Wall, a short separate cliff with several corners and a prominent roof. Right of the Dihedral Wall, across a tree-filled gully, is the Shield, a broad, rounded, slabby area of rock. Right from Roger's Corner, the wall rears vertical, with obvious features including the arches of Frog Pond and Sagittarius, the long flake of Japanese Gardens, and the striking thin crack of City Park. Right of City Park is the Narrow Arrow, a detached "pinnacle," 250 feet above the talus. This area of the cliff, from City Park to the quarry scar, is characterized by numerous vertical thin cracks split by several horizontal ledge systems. Farther right, the rock deteriorates.

Immediately right of the Lower Wall is a broad talus field. There are several large boulders, with some interesting (scary!) bouldering. Much of this talus is unstable, however, so take care not to get squished. The quarry wall presently has only two routes (both A3, see Orc Tower photo), and those are on the far right, where the rock is more stable. A massive rockfall occured during the winter of 1982, further destabilizing this area.

On the right margin of the quarry scar is Orc Tower, a distinct, castle-shaped tower. Right of this is the Country, an area of knobby, steep faces and weathered cracks which was somehow spared the quarryman's drill. National attention has recently been focused on this area, not for the rock climbing, but for physics experiments seeking the Fifth Force. A large cave was bored several hundred feet into the wall. Luckily, it did not destroy any existing routes. Since then, numerous new routes have been established here. The Country and Orc Tower may and should be reached from a road paralleling the railroad tracks, and reaching the cave door.

A trail leads left from the Lower Wall, reaching the Garden Wall shortly. The Garden Wall may also be reached directly from the railroad tracks. Farther left is a prominent, forested dome, the Lower Lump. The right side of this formation is an overhanging, blocky wall. The left side is a clean slab bordered by overhangs. The Wart (or Lowest Lump) is a small dome lying directly in front of the Lower Lump.

A trail leads upwards from the Garden Wall, passing the "K" Cliff (a short cliff on the right) to the notch between the Lower Lump and the Lower Wall mass. This is the Inner Wall, a narrow canyon with numerous crack and face routes, and much potential. This area has the advantage of being much cooler than the Lower Wall on summer days, but conversely, it is wet and cold on moderate spring and fall days.

Descent routes will be discussed within the text, with the area where they are likely to be used.

The first pitch of Iron Horse, Lower Town Wall

THE SLAB AREA – LEFT SIDE

The Slab Area, or Great Northern Slab, has many of the easiest as well as several of the most difficult routes at Index. This area is characterized by cracks, overhangs, and a broad slab. A dark, dirty wall flanks the slab on the left. Descent is best accomplished by rappel. One long rappel from the tree at the top, beside **Leo Chimney**, and then another from the Railroad Bolts will reach the base of the cliff. There is a good anchor at the top of **Libra Crack** as well.

1. **LEO CHIMNEY** (– ★★) **5.6**
   The deep lefthand chimney. Dirty, with loose blocks. Protection and rating questionable. FA: unknown.

2. **VELVASHEEN** ★ **5.6**
   A left-curving arch. Protection to 3". Deserves to be more popular. FA: Mark Weigelt, Cheryl Greenman, 1969.

3. **ARCHIES** **5.6**
   A right-facing arch starting from Velvasheen. Continue up through a dihedral/ roof to the upper slab. Protection to 3". FA: unknown.

4. **GREAT NORTHERN SLAB** ★★ **5.6**
   This route takes the twin thin cracks above the railroad bolts. Continue up a corner to the upper slab. Protection to 2". FA: Paul Guimarin, Philip Leatherman 1965.

5. **LIBRA CRACK (aka PISCES)** ★★★ **5.10a**
   An overhanging hand crack. This route technically begins with the difficult dihedral boulder problem (5.10) and climbs the easy crack/trough to the upper crack. From the bolt belay, traverse left to a dihedral finish. Protection to 3". FA: Mark Weigelt, Mike Berman, 1969.

6. **TAURUS** ★★ **5.7**
   From the block right of Libra, climb up and right, under the big roof, then through a short overhang to a thin crack. Protection to 2". FA: Dave Anderson, Rich Carlstad, Carla Firey, Donn Heller, 1972.

7. **BLOCKBUSTER** ★ **5.9**
   The curving "Sickle Crack" left of Aries' dihedral, through the overhanging block. Protection to 2". FA: Ron Burgner, Thom Nephew, 1970.

8. **THE LIZARD (aka ARIES)** ★★★ **5.8**
   Take the obvious, short exfoliated fist crack to a large ledge. Continue up a corner, a chimney, and pass the big overhang on the left. Protection to 3". FA: Ron Burgner, Thom Nephew, 1970.

9. **LET'S GO BOWLING** **5.10d**
   This is the short arete left of the exfoliated fist crack. A bolt protects this 20-foot "pitch". FA: Jim Yoder, Matt Kerns 1988.

10. **VOYAGE TO THE BOTTOM OF THE VERGE (aka ON THE VIRGIN)** **5.10d (R/ X)**
    The outside corner right of Aries' dihedral. Protection should include a #2½ Friend. Rated R or X if fixed pin is missing. FA: Greg Olson, John Nelson, Mark Boatsman, 1982.

11. **ON THE VERGE** ★ **5.11b/c**
    The arete right of Aries' chimney. Fixed protection. Both **Voyage** and the **Verge** can be connected in one pitch. FLA: Dan Lepeska, 1980.

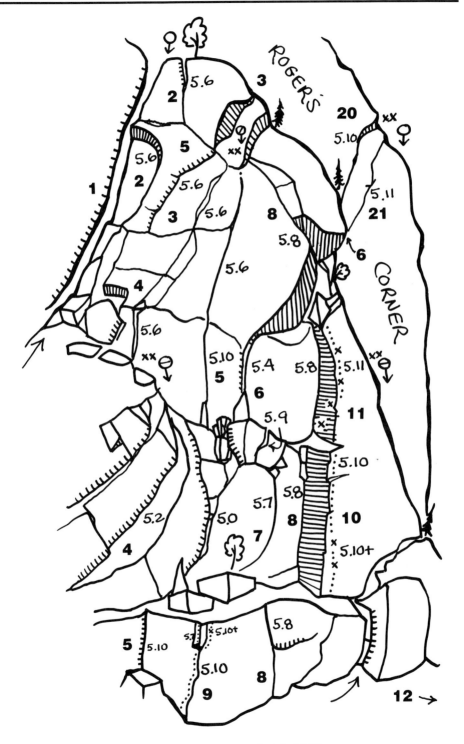

GREAT NORTHERN SLAB AREA

12. **CRYSTALLINE 5.8+** (not shown)
Right of Aries' fist crack, along the trail to the lower wall, is an obvious arete boulder problem. Above this is a large block with a horizontal crack. Climb this crack and the short arete/face above. Protection to 1"; include a #1 Friend. FA: Doug Weaver 1986.

SLAB AREA and ROGER'S CORNER – RIGHT SIDE

The right side of the Slab is generally unbroken, except for a few cracks and noticeable overhangs. There is occasional minor rockfall in this area, frequently caused by other climbers. This slab is reached by scrambling from either side. Roger's Corner is the large dihedral on the right side of the slab. Descend via rappel from various anchors in the corner, or at the top of Breakfast of Champions.

13. **WALKIN' THE DOG 5.10c AO**
The leftmost bolt line leads to a thin, friable crack. Protection to 1". FA: Don Brooks, 1980.

14. **SONIC REDUCER ★★ 5.12b/c**
A water-worn slab, protected by a line of bolts. Rappel from bolt anchors on the left. 5.10+ AO if you aid the first three bolts. FA: John Nelson, 1984.

15. **TERMINAL PREPPIE ★★★ 5.11c (PG-13)**
Right of Sonic Reducer is a roof leading to a steep, bolt-protected slab through a second roof. Belay at the base of Nick O'Time. Small wired nuts. FA: Greg Olson, John Nelson, 1983.

16. **NICK O' TIME 5.10a**
A curving corner right of Taurus' thin crack. A short step-across (5.8) from Taurus most easily reaches this. Protection to 2". A good finish for Terminal Preppie. FA: Don Brooks, Steve VanMowrick, 1980.

17. **STRENGTH THROUGH BOWLING (–★) 5.11a (R)**
A poorly protected line, climbing a roof and poor cracks right of Terminal Preppie. Small wired nuts. Rappel from fixed pins in the overhang above (if they are there), or else continue left up Terminal Preppie. FA: Greg Olson, 1983.

18. **ROGER'S CORNER 5.9**
The obvious huge dihedral. Protection to 3". Ends at the base of Breakfast of Champions. FA: Greg Donaldson, Roger Johnson, Richard Mathies, 1967.

19. **SUGAR BEAR 5.10c**
Thin cracks right of the start of Roger's Corner. Friable rock. Protection to 1". FA: Don Brooks 1980.

20. **BREAKFAST OF CHAMPIONS ★★★ 5.10a**
The steep lefthand crack above Roger's Corner. Protection to 3". Rappel anchors at the top. FA: Dave Anderson and Don Harder or Julie Brugger and Carla Firey (without tree).

21. **MARGINAL KARMA (aka Windmills) ★ 5.11b**
The righthand thin crack. Friable rock. Protection to 2". FA: Don Brooks (TR); FLA: Dan Lepeska 1983.

22. **VIRGIN ON THE RIDICULOUS ★ 5.11d**
This route starts in a dihedral right of Sugar Bear and ascends the impressive arete right of Roger's Corner. The cruxes are said to be well protected; however, some of the rock is loose. Belay at the edge of the arete, then a short pitch leads to the top. Protection to 1". FA: Greg Child 1987.

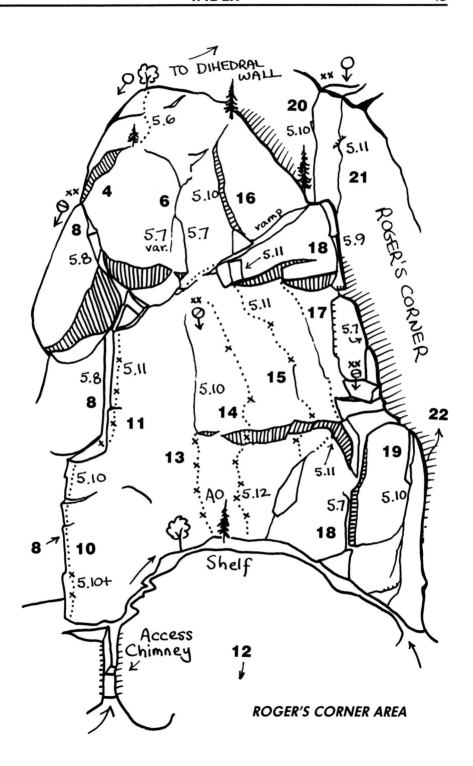

ROGER'S CORNER AREA

DIHEDRAL WALL

Directly above **Roger's Corner**, left across a gully from the **Shield**, is this short wall, having a number of steep dihedrals and an obvious overhang. The best approach is probably from the **Slab**.

1. **TERMINATOR**   ★★ **5.10a**
   Bolted slab, cracks on left side. FA: Doug Weaver, Jeff Wright, 1988.
2. **DEFOLIATOR**   **5.7**
   Crack right of **Terminator** leading to dihedral and face. Protection to 2". FA: Doug Weaver, Scott Prueter, Jeff Wright, 1988.
3. **INSTIGATOR**   **5.8**
   Right, around corner from **Defoliator**, a blocky arete leads to an open book. Protection to 1½". FA: Jeff Wright, Doug Weaver, 1988.
4. **CUP & SAUCER**   ★★★ **5.11c**
   Dihedral leading to roof. A direct and better start to **Julie's Roof**. A stemming testpiece. FA: John Nelson, Darryl Cramer 1985.
5. **JULIE'S ROOF**   ★ **5.11a**
   The middle corner, very obvious because of the large overhang at mid-height. This route passes the roof on the right to enter a steep corner. Protection to 2". FA: Julie Brugger, Tom Hargis, 1983.
6. **GOGUM**   ★ **5.11**
   The right-hand dihedral. Protection to 2". FA: Greg Olson, Greg McKenna, 1984.

LOWER TOWN WALL – THE TERRACE

The **Terrace** is the grassy slope atop the final pitches of **Princely Ambitions** and **Tadpole**. It can be reached via a trail from the top of the **Slab** area or from the top of **Breakfast of Champions**. The best way to descend from the **Terrace** is by rappelling down **Breakfast** and **Roger's Corner**. Two 165-foot ropes just reach the ground. This rappel overhangs its entire distance. At the back of the **Terrace** lies the **Dihedral Wall** and to the right is **The Shield**.

LOWER TOWN WALL – LEFT SIDE

The left side of the **Lower Wall** has a number of steep crack routes, both free and aid. The most prominent features of this area are the arches of **Frog Pond** and **Sagittarius**. The steep flake first pitch of **Princely Ambitions** is also noticeable. Rappelling either **Princely Ambitions** or **Roger's Corner** is the best method of descent.

1. **SNOW WHITE**   **5.11c A2+**
   The leftmost route, starting as a thin aid crack (A2+). From the ledge, keep right up a slanting crack under a roof. Hooks and rurps plus numerous to 1". There are variations to either pitch, both keeping left. FA: Rich Carlstad, Dale Hardisty, 1972.
2. **ALL-PURPOSE DUCK**   ★ **5.11c (PG-13)**
   Climb the dirty corner left of **Snow White** until it is possible to traverse right, past an old bolt, into **Snow White**. Continue up **Snow White** (crux) until it is possible to veer right into **Princely Ambitions**. The crux may be protected by tied off **Lost Arrows**, the only pitons needed. FA: Terry Lien, 1984.
3. **PRINCELY AMBITIONS**   ★ **5.8**
   The steep flake right of **Snow White**. The second pitch is a wide corner. Protection to 2". FA: Clint Cummins, Jeremy Metz, 1977.

Dihedral Wall

The Shield

The Terrace

var.

Roger's Corner

ROGER'S CORNER AREA

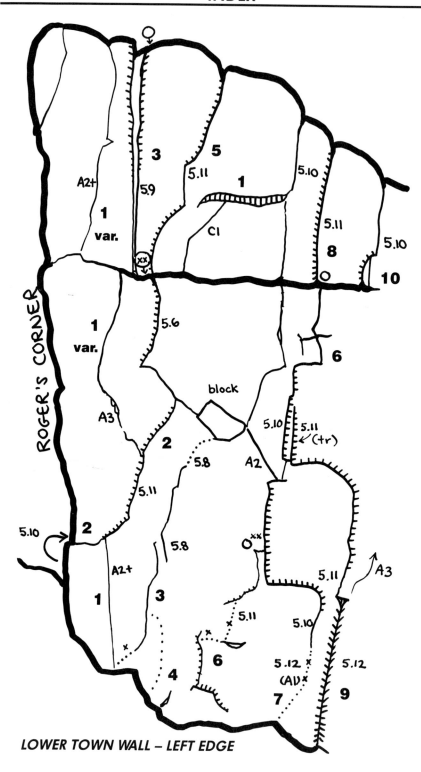

LOWER TOWN WALL – LEFT EDGE

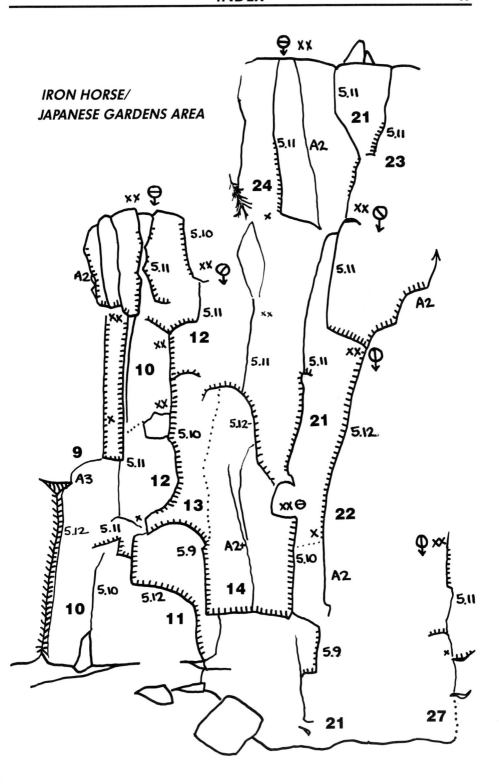

IRON HORSE/
JAPANESE GARDENS AREA

4. **GO FOR A SODA**   **5.10b**
Direct start to Princely Ambitions. Bolts, RPs. FA: Nicola Masciandaro, Darryl Cramer, 1985.

5. **DOCTOR SNIFF AND THE TUNA BOATERS** ★★ **5.11a**
From the ledge belay on Princely Ambitions, climb the short righthand arch to a thin crack, which leads to a flaring chimney. Protection to 2", including RPs and Friends. FA: Terry Lien, Greg Olson, 1983.

6. **MODEL WORKER** ★ **5.11b**
A bolted face climb which reaches the arch of Frog Pond. Continue up the corner to a belay at the base of Tadpole (5.10c). Bolts and a fixed pin protect the hardest sections; a Friend is recommended for the corner. This can be done in one 140-foot pitch. FA: Greg Olson, John Nelson, 1982 (first pitch); Terry Lien, Greg Olsen, Max Dufford, 1988 (complete).

7. **FROG POND**   **5.12b A2**
Hook moves and bolts (goes free at 5.12) reach the arch, which leads to a bolted belay in the corner (the belay of Model Worker). FA: Dave Anderson, John Teasdale, 1971; FFA: Greg Olson, 1988.

8. **TADPOLE**   ★★ **5.11d**
This is the original third pitch of Frog Pond, a difficult thin corner crack. Protection to 1", including RPs. FFA: Terry Lien, John Nelson.

9. **NUMBAH TEN** ★ **5.12b and/or A3**
Right of the start of Frog Pond is this diedre leading to a roof and cracks. The aid route goes right and up the second corner to the left edge of Iron Horse belay ledge (140', some loose rock near ledge). The free version goes straight up and left in an obvious corner. Bolts, protection to 1" (free version). FA: Dave Anderson, Donn Heller, 1974; FFA: Max Dufford (variation), 1988.

10. **IRON HORSE**   ★★ **5.12a**
Right of Numbah Ten, starting at a protruding flake, is a thin crack system leading through a roof. Continue right up cracks from the ledge. Protection to 1", including pins for the upper pitch. Most parties climb to Ringing Flake and rappel (5.11d). FA: Roger Johnson, Doug Leen (to 140'); Kit Hanes, Bob Langenbach, 1969; FFA: Peter Croft (to flake), 1981; Dick Cilley (to 140'), 1984.

11. **ARACHNID ARCH**   ★ **5.12a (PG-13)**
This is the short, thin arch right of Iron Horse. RPs, TCU's, other thin crack protection. FFA: Dick Cilley (toprope), 1982; FLA: Jeff Smoot, 1986.

12. **SAGITTARIUS**   ★★★ **5.11b**
The obvious wide arch right of Iron Horse, leading to a steep flake. The route has been free climbed past the upper overhang to join Iron Horse at the ledge. Protection to 4" (pitons above upper ledge). FA: Pat Timson (to flake); Mark Moore (to roof), 1974; Terry Lien (to ledge), 1982.

13. **TANTRIC BAZOOKA** ★★ **5.11c/d (R)**
From dihedral on Sagittarius (20 feet off ground), strike rightward onto steep face, up flakes and cracks. From right end of roof, face and shallow cracks reach a belay at the base of Chopper Flake. Questionable, hard-to-place protection; RPs, TCUs. FA: Greg Collum, Greg Child 1988.

Narrow Arrow

15
16
14
18
21
17
19
14
19
10
12
20
8
25
35
21
26
9
29
30
10
12
24
23
33
14
34
21
28
30
58

THE SHIELD AREA

14. **TEN-PERCENT METEOROLOGICAL VINCULATION** ★★★ IV, 5.11d A2+ (or 5.12a)

Right of Sagittarius is a very thin crack system which leads to the upper shield, and continues to the top of the wall. Numerous, to 2". The first pitch is aided (A2+); the remaining pitches have been climbed free. The route can be done all free via a traverse in from Japanese Gardens. FA: Dave Anderson, Bruce Carson, 1974; FFA: Larry Kemp (traverse variation), Darryl Cramer (3rd and 4th pitches), 1987. Free protection unknown.

THE SHIELD

The Shield is a blank, rounded upper section of the wall directly right of a very obvious arch. The upper pitch of Ten-Percent climbs incipient cracks near the center of the Shield.

15. **LAMAR'S TRUST**   **5.9**

A face pitch right of the gully separating the Dihedral formation with the Shield, just left of Beak, Beak, Beak. Start on flakes to reach the bolt-protected face. Protection to 2". FA: Greg McKenna, Greg Olson, 1982.

16. **BEAK, BEAK, BEAK**   **5.9**

This is the long corner/arch on the upper left side of the Shield. Exit left in a crack halfway up. Protection to 4". FA: Greg Olsen, John Nelson, 1982.

17. **NEWEST INDUSTRY**   ★★★ **5.11b**

Slab route on left edge of Shield proper. This is a classic Index friction climb. It may join Ten-Percent for a second pitch to the top of the cliff. Bolts. FA: Darryl Cramer, Greg Olsen, Terry Lien, 1987.

18. **JOURNEY TO PITAR**   ★ **5.12a**

From the top of the third pitch of Ten-Percent, this right-hand friction climb joins Japanese Gardens. FA: Greg Olsen, Darryl Cramer, 1988.

19. **CHEESEBURGERS ON TRIAL**   **5.11b**

This is a curving rib right of Ten-Percent. FA: Terry Lien, 1984 (TR); FLA: Greg Olsen, Darryl Cramer, Terry Lien, 1988.

20. **STIFF KITTENS**   ★★ **5.11d**

A diagonal crack left of Japanese Gardens' third pitch. The first 50' are continuously difficult. The crux is an undercling left across a roof into Cheeseburgers. Protection to 2". FA: Darryl Cramer, Greg Olsen 1987.

LOWER TOWN WALL – CENTRAL SECTION

21. **JAPANESE GARDENS** ★★★★ **5.11c (PG-13)**
A "long" free route starting right of Ten-Percent, climbing the flake and cracks to reach the top of the wall. Protection to 4", including Friends and small nuts. There may be a substantial runout on the final pitch. FA: Lowell Anderson, Dave Page, Jim Stoddard, 1968; FFA: John Nelson, Terry Lien, 1984.

22. **STERN FARMER** ★★ **5.12c, A2+**
A shallow slot right of the first pitch of Japanese Gardens, which continues right past an overhang, rejoining Japanese Gardens near the Park Benches. First pitch goes free via traverse in from Japanese Gardens, with clean protection. Nuts and pins to 2". FFA: Terry Lien (1st pitch) 1984.

23. **TROUT FARM MASSACRE** **5.11b**
A variation of the second pitch of Japanese Gardens, continuing straight up where the original route curves slightly left. Protection to 1". FA: John Nelson, Terry Lien 1983.

24. **IT'S A DOG'S LIFE BUT YOU CAN PICNIC WITH US** ★ **5.11c (PG-13)**
Another variation of the second pitch, taking a left-hand corner. Thin pitons are needed for protection. Beside it, to the right, is an A2+ crack variation. FFA: Terry Lien, John Nelson, 1983.

25. **KLAUS VON BULOW AND THE ALGORITHM OF LOVE** **5.10c (PG-13)**
Finger crack right of third pitch of Japanese Gardens leads to a shallow corner and a roof. Protection to 2"; HB nuts recommended. FA: Greg Olsen, Darryl Cramer, 1988.
Variation: Trapped by a Hamster 5.10c Continue right from edge of roof. Small wired nuts. FA: Greg Olsen, Larry Kemp, 1988.

26. **GIANT-SIZE BABY THING** **5.11a (PG-13)**
Corner just left of Slow Children. Protection to 2"; include TCUs, Rollers. FA: Greg Olsen, Darryl Cramer 1988.

27. **BWANA DICK** **5.11 (PG-13/R)**
A poorly protected pitch right of the start of Japanese Gardens. RPs needed for protection. FA: Dick Cilley, David Rosenfeld, 1984.

28. **ARTIFICE (aka BAT SKINS)** ★ **5.12a**
A rightward undercling just left of City Park leads to a belay 50 feet off the ground; the route continues up a shallow corner to a knobby face. Traverse left to a questionable belay. Continue left to cracks and up. The crux on the second pitch (5.11d) can be avoided by using the flake/crack to the right (5.11b). This will be the third pitch if you belay after 50 feet. FA: Bruce Carson, Pat Timson, Dave Andersen, 1971; FFA: Darryl Cramer, Max Dufford, Nicola Masciandaro, 1986.

29. **GOLD BAR GIRLS** ★ **5.9+**
From the first belay of City Park, traverse down and left until flakes lead up. People seem to either really like or really despise this climb. Protection to 1½". FA: Max Dufford, Dante Leonardi, 1984.

30. **CITY PARK** ★★★ **III, 5.13c C1**
The very obvious initial thin crack leads to a ledge at 120' (5.13 or C1). Another pitch leads to the Park Benches, where a right-arching crack (C1) leads to an obvious dirty dihedral with a tree. Nuts and Friends to 2", including many smaller wired pieces for the first pitch. One may rappel the route. FA: Roger Johnson, Richard Mathies, 1966; FFA: Todd Skinner (1st pitch), 1986.

The Terrace →

14

21

23

24

Chopper
Flake →

21

28

29

30

32

33

34

36

38

22

40

36

27

21

33

37

31

28

30

28

CITY PARK AREA

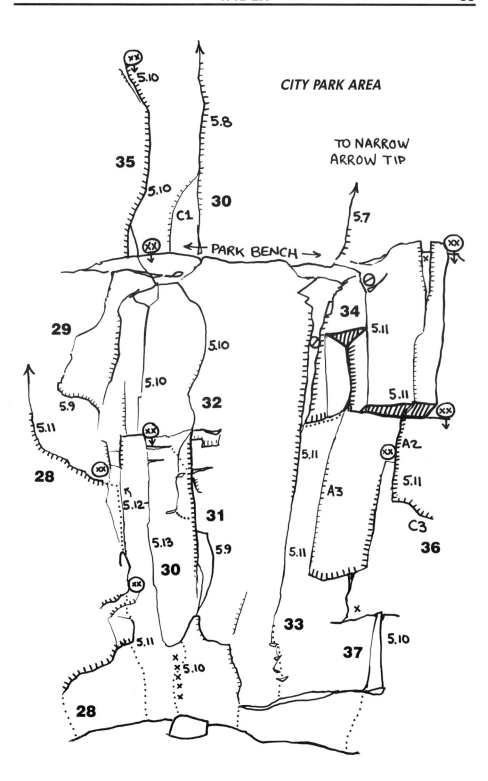

CITY PARK AREA

TO NARROW
ARROW TIP

31. **GODZILLA** ★★★ **5.9**
Climb flakes in a corner and a thin crack paralleling City Park on the right. Protection to 3", including Friends. FA: Don Harder, Donn Heller, 1972.
32. **LEAPIN' LIZARDS** **5.10b**
From City Park belay ledge, traverse right back into Godzilla dihedral and up crack to Park Benches. May be dirty. Protection to 2". FA: Greg Olson, Russell Erickson 1983.
33. **DEAL WITH IT RANGER** **5.11a (PG-13)**
Right of Godzilla is this shallow corner leading to a flaring chimney. Protection to 1", including RPs. FA: Dick Cilley, John Nelson, Darryl Cramer, 1984.
34. **NATURAL LOG CABIN** ★★ **5.11c/d**
From Ranger's dihedral, traverse right into corner on prow and up crack. This route is much harder if you are short. Two ropes are recommended to reduce rope drag at the top. Protection to 1½". FA: Darryl Cramer, Nicola Masciandaro, 1985.
35. **SLOW CHILDREN** ★★★ **5.10d**
From the Park Bench, just left of City Park, is this superb flared corner with a thin crack. The pitch ends at a rappel anchor. Protection to 1", including several wired nuts. FA: John Carpentar and party, 1980.

LOWER WALL - NARROW ARROW AREA

The Narrow Arrow Area, on the far right side of the Lower Wall, is perhaps the most crack-intensive section of the cliff. The Narrow Arrow Pinnacle is the small protrusion high above the lower overhangs, with a noticeable off-width. A rappel route bears rightward, following the Narrow Arrow route. A standard rappel route from the ledge below the Narrow Arrow follows the Direct route.

36. **NARROW ARROW OVERHANG** ★ **II, 5.11d C3**
This route climbs through the large overhang directly below the Narrow Arrow. A short corner leads to an arch and a crack beneath the roof (C3). The overhang itself has been led free (crux). Above, traverse ledges left to a brushy corner which leads to the Narrow Arrow notch. Nuts to 2", with many smaller sizes. FA: Greg Donaldson, Richard Mathies, 1968; FFA: Dick Cilley (roof), 1984.
Variation: A shallow corner on the left leads to Natural Log Cabin's corner (said to be A3+).
37. **STRAIGHT ARROW** **5.11b**
A direct first pitch of Narrow Arrow Overhang leading up a corner and half-chimney to a bolt belay 30 feet below an overhang. Protection to 3". Double ropes recommended. FFA: Darryl Cramer, John Nelson, 1985.
38. **NARROW ARROW DIRECT (aka THE CLEFT)** ★★ **5.11b A2**
Begin right of Narrow Arrow Overhang, up 5.11b corner (fixed pins), then aid to a ledge (A2). The remainder of the route is free, taking the dihedral, overhangs, and an offwidth to a broad ledge just below the Narrow Arrow summit. Protection to 6", including pins for the first pitch. FA: Ron Burgner, Mark Weigelt, 1970; FFA: John Stoddard (second and third pitches), 1979.
39. **SOCIAL VACUUM** ★ **5.11b**
This is the horizontal thin crack going rightward from just below the 5.10 offwidth of Narrow Arrow Direct. Protection to 1". FA: Dick Cilley, Greg Olsen, 1984.

40. **SHIRLEY (aka BURIED TREASURE)** ★ **5.11c**
Right of the start of Direct, climb a white arch and a steep corner to cracks and the upper shelf. Take crack right of Freedom Fighter to top (this crack is Buried Treasure). Protection to 2", including Friends. A classic stemming problem. FA: Don Brooks; FFA: Dick Cilley, John Nelson, Greg Olsen, 1984.

41. **I'D RATHER BE GOLFING** ★ **5.10d**
The leftmost of two intimate cracks right of dihedral of Narrow Arrow Direct. Protection to 2". FA: John Nelson, Terry Lien, 1983.

42. **CLUBHOUSE SCENE** ★ **5.10b**
This is the right-most of the two cracks previously mentioned. Protection to 2". FA: Terry Lien, John Nelson 1983.

43. **FREEDOM FIGHTER** **5.10d**
At the top of Shirley, on the left, is this dirty flake. Continue up to a steep corner to join Hard as Hell. Cleaned, this would be a good route. Protection to 3". FA: Don Brooks, Art Kampen, 1981.

44. **THIN FINGERS** ★★★ **5.11a**
The highly obvious parallel cracks right of Shirley, reaching a rappel anchor in one pitch (80') from the ledge. Protection to 2", including Friends. FFA: Paul Boving 1976.

45. **BIG TOES** ★ **5.11c**
Right variation of Thin Fingers. Some people use two ropes and place one piece high up in Thin Fingers before traversing. Protection to 2". Bring plenty of small nuts for this climb. FA: Darryl Cramer, Greg Olsen, 1986.

46. **24-HOUR BUCCANEER** ★ **5.11b (R)** (not shown)
A short crack and face below Thin Fingers leads to dihedral and Thin Fingers' ledge. This scary route has seen some long falls, so be careful. Protection includes RPs. FA: Terry Lien, John Nelson, Greg Olsen, 1985. First groundfall: Nicola Masciandaro.

47. **DEATH TO ZEKE** ★★ **5.11d (PG-13)**
An arch high on the right side of the Narrow Arrow. Protection to 2", including RPs, TCUs. FA: Terry Lien, John Nelson, 1984.

48. **HARD AS HELL** **5.10**
A variation taking the arch and off-width crack just right of Zeke which is not especially recommended. Protection to 5". FA: Don Harder, Donn Heller, 1974.

NARROW ARROW AREA

LOWER WALL - QUARRY AREA

On the far right, left of the huge talus slope, is this section of the wall. Steep, angular cracks predominate the climbing in this area. The rock deteriorates as one moves farther right. There are numerous rappel anchors in place on the various ledges, making a descent from almost anywhere possible.

49. **FREE AT LAST   5.10b**
    This long route starts with a shallow chimney, leading to a long dihedral and crack pitch with an off-width. Higher, an easy ramp leads to steep cracks and a short face. Protection to 3". A variation reaches the noticeable flaring corner high up, via A2 cracks, adding an additional pitch to this long route. FA: Ron Burgner, Mark Weigelt; FFA: Mead Hargis, Jim Langdon.

50. **TATOOSH   5.10b**
    Climb Free at Last to a steep dihedral left of the off-width second pitch of that route. Protection to 2". FA: unknown.

51. **SLAM   5.11c (PG-13)**
    Right of the ramp on Tatoosh are these discontinuous cracks leading past a ledge to a steep corner crack. Protection to 1". FA: Terry Lien, John Nelson 1984.

52. **LET'S BARBECUE   ★★ 5.11c**
    A steep crack climb up a shallow corner on a prow. Protection to 1". FA: Terry Lien, John Nelson, 1984.

53. **BOB & DORIS   5.10c**
    Right of the upper half of Slam is this steep, albeit dirty corner. Protection to 1". FA: Terry Lien, John Nelson, 1983.

54. **TAI & RANDI MEMORIAL   5.10d**
    A corner and roof climb right of Let's Barbecue. Protection to 3". FA: Kjell Swedin, Bob McDougall 1980.

55. **JUST SAY NO2   5.12 A0**
    This is the arete left of Walter B, with many bolts. FA: Jim Yoder 1988.

56. **WITH APOLOGIES TO WALTER B.   5.11b (PG- 13)**
    A steep thin crack in a corner, splitting a pillar left of the Quarry Crack, reached via rubbish and a difficult traverse. Protection to 2". FA: Kjell Swedin; FFA: Dan Lepeska, 1980.

57. **QUARRY CRACK   5.9**
    Right of Walter B. is this obvious off-width in a corner. Protection to 3". FA: Don Harder, Donn Heller 1973.

58. **NARROW ARROW   (−★) 5.7**
    The easiest way of reaching the Narrow Arrow summit, taking a pitch of shattered rock on the far right to the initial shelf. Not recommended. FA: Who cares?

59. **PREYING MANTLE   5.10c**
    This is a short arching crack on the extreme right of the Lower Wall. May have been "destroyed" by rockfall. Protection to 2". FA: Dave Anderson, Kjell Swedin, Cal Folsom, 1980.

LOWER WALL - ORC TOWER

Orc Tower is the obvious detached pillar on the right side of the hideous quarried wall. The route starts on the left to reach this esteemed summit. There is an aid route left of Orc Tower (A3, see photo), with two variations, the only ventures on the quarried wall since the major rockfall of 1982.

1. **ORC TOWER   5.10d A3**
   Start on the left side by climbing Patrick's Flake (5.10d). The route takes the left corner/chimney, via cracks and tricky aid. The tower appears to have numerous precarious blocks poised and waiting. Numerous to 3". FA: unknown.
2. **REBEL (RUBBLE?) WITHOUT A CAUSE   5.11b**
   On the west face of Orc Tower. Start near the Savage Garden belay, up a blocky chimney; the second pitch traverses right from the chimney to a crack just left of the prow. Routefinding is troublesome. Protection to 3". FA: Greg Child, Greg Collum, 1988.
3. **STEEL MONKEY   ★ 5.12b/c (C1)** (not shown)
   Thin crack and face left of Patrick's Flake. This short crack can be easily aided to set up a top rope; however, do not use pitons as the rock is very brittle. Protection to 1". FA: Brooke Sandahl, 1987.
4. **CROWBAR   5.11a** (not shown)
   Three bolts lead up to a thin crack through two roofs right of Steel Monkey. FA: Darryl Cramer, Max Dufford 1987.
5. **TED NUGENT IN A BASKET   5.11b** (not shown)
   Left of Patrick's Flake, eight bolts lead to a tree. The crux is getting past the third bolt. Fixed protection. FA: Greg Olsen, Darryl Cramer, Max Dufford 1987.
6. **PATRICK'S FLAKE   5.10d**
   Originally this was part of the outside face route on Orc Tower. Protection is hard to place. FA: Patrick?; FFA: Terry Lien?
7. **TOTAL SEAWASH CALYPSO   ★ 5.11d** (not shown)
   This route starts in the roof right of Patrick's Flake. The second bolt is difficult to clip; consider bringing a cheat stick so the crux is not clipping a bolt. Fixed protection. FA: Darryl Cramer, Greg Olsen, John Nelson, Larry Kemp, 1988.
8. **WILLING SLAVE   5.11d** (not shown)
   This climb begins 30 feet right of Seawash. It joins Savage Garden for 20 feet and then splits off to the left. This climb is marred by an extremely dirty finish. FA: Greg Collum, Greg Child, 1988.
9. **SAVAGE GARDEN   5.11b (PG-13)**
   Starts just to the right of Willing Slave. This route has some sections of poor rock. Bring some of the smallest nuts available to minimize the runouts. FA: Greg Collum, Greg Child, 1987.
10. **KITE FLYING BLIND   ★★★ 5.11b/c (PG-13)**
    This climb starts 50 feet left of the first pitch of Zoom. The first pitch (Elvis-Nixon, 5.11a) is slightly runout after the crux. The second pitch (crux) ascends flakes right of Wipe to an easy crack. Protection to 2". FA: Greg Collum, Greg Child (first pitch); Greg Collum (2nd), 1988.

11. **THE FLY**   **5.10+** **(TR)** (not shown)
Left and uphill from the start of **Zoom** is this very short top-rope problem, passing a small overhang. **Kite Flying** begins just right of this. FA: Terry Lien, John Nelson, 1980.

12. **WIPE**   ★★★ **5.11a (PG-13)**
Right of Orc Tower is this surprisingly good crack and face pitch. Access is by rappel or the first pitch of **Kite Flying Blind**, unless you are willing to climb the loose lower section of this wall (5.7?). It is also possible to traverse left from **Zoom** (5.10d). The climb can be located from below by finding **The Fly**. Protection to 1", include RPs. FA: John Nelson, Terry Lien 1984.

13. **THE FIFTH FORCE**   **5.10c (TR)** (not shown)
A face/slab on a large boulder hidden in the vicinity of **Zoom**. The original Fifth Force. FA: Rick Graham 1984.

14. **ZOOM**   ★★★ **5.10d (PG-13)**
A knobby face climb left of the cave door at the Country. The first pitch starts directly above a concrete well. The first and third pitches are obvious and recommended; the second lead is heavily vegetated. Protection to 3", with RPs and Friends recommended. FA: John Nelson, Steve Strong, 1983.

ORC TOWER

LOWER WALL - THE COUNTRY

The Country is located at the farthest right margin of the Lower Wall, above the broad graded area, and near the iron door of the cave. The routes here are concentrated in sections of good rock.

15. **CHARGED PARTICLE (aka WHAM!)** ★ **5.11b/c (R)**
A righthand variation to Zoom's first pitch. Mostly fixed protection. Watch out for rope drag. FA: Greg Collum, 1985.

16. **LITTLE JUPITER** **5.11d/12a**
Short dihedral and face left of start of Big Science. FA: Jim Purdy, Greg Olsen, Max Dufford, 1988.

17. **BIG SCIENCE** **5.12a**
This is the short, bolt protected face left of the cave. It is easily toproped by climbing Ultrabrutal. Protection to ½". FA: Greg Child, 1985.

18. **SCIENTIFIC AMERICANS** **5.12d**
Climb knobby face directly above Big Science. Bolts. FA: Greg Child, Geoff Weigand 1988.

19. **CONDITIONED RESPONSE** **5.11a**
Starts at bolts 20 feet right of the end of Scientific Americans. Goes up and right over roofs. Easiest access is by rappel. Protection to 2½". FA: Greg Collum, Dan Cauthorn, 1988.

20. **ULTRABRUTAL** **5.7**
Climb a right-leaning crack system imediately left of the cave until it is possible to traverse left to the top of Big Science. FA: unknown.

21. **CUNNING STUNT** ★ **5.11a**
This two pitch route begins immediately right of the cave. The first pitch ends at the end of an orange arch; the second at a tree directly above. Protection to 2". FA: Greg Child, 1983.

22. **THE FIFTH FORCE** ★★★ **5.12b**
An excellent steep, bolted face climb, not to be confused with the shorter toprope problem peviously listed. Begin behind the big tree right of the cave and climb up face and corners to chain anchor. Mostly fixed protection, but bring along some small nuts, too. FA: Greg Collum, Greg Child, 1987.

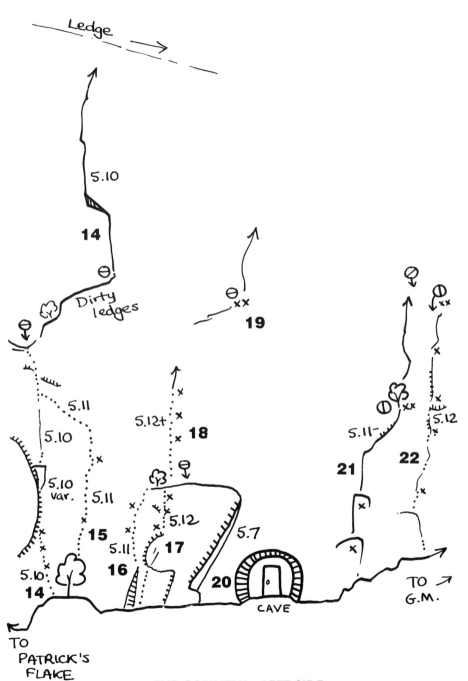

THE COUNTRY – LEFT SIDE

23. **SPOONER** ★ **5.11d**
This tricky route, right of Fifth Force, begins with an overhanging hand traverse. Fixed protection. FA: John Nelson, Darryl Cramer, 1983.

24. **FOOL'S GOLD** **5.9**
This is a slab/face up a gold-colored wall, above the first pitch of Heart of the Country. It begins atop the same flake as Heart of the Country. Protection to 1". FA: Don Brooks, Chris Syrjala, 1980.

25. **HEART OF THE COUNTRY** ★★★ **5.11b (R)**
An excellent three pitch route starting from a large, detached flake right of Spooner. Climb a block and unprotected slab (5.10) to a ledge, then steep cracks to the top, staying right of G.M. after the second pitch. Protection to 2". Most parties avoid the initial, unprotected pitch. FA: John Stoddard, 1980.

26. **G.M.** ★ **5.9**
Start up a brushy corner to a ledge. Steep, wide cracks continue past an overhang to a large dihedral/chimney. Protection to 4". Rappelling the route is the most expedient method of descent for this and for Heart of the Country. FA: Greg Markov, Ed Gibson, 1973.

27. **PHONE CALLS FROM THE DEAD** ★ **5.11b**
A face climb just right of G.M., taking a knobby wall to a belay/rappel anchor in the middle of nowhere. Fixed protection, but maybe include RPs. FA: Greg Olsen, John Nelson, 1983.

28. **WHIPPED CREAM** **5.11d** (not shown)
Bolted wall left of Dead Bobcats. Clip first bolt from a tree. FA: Greg Olsen, Max Dufford, John Nelson, Jim Purdy, 1988.

29. **DEAD BOBCATS TRAVEL WEST** **5.9** (not shown)
Right and up a bit from G.M., is this steep, wide flake pitch, with some vegetation. Protection to 3". FA: John Marts, 1969.

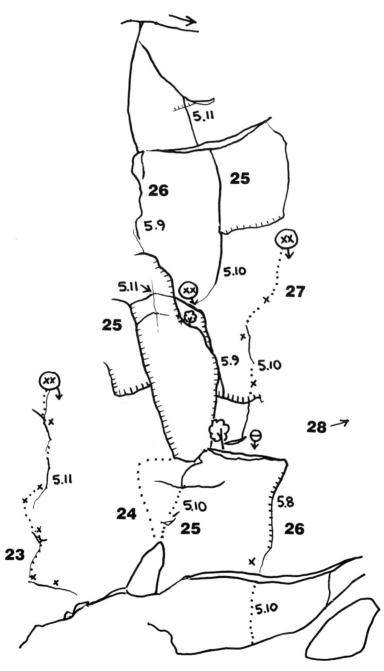

THE COUNTRY – RIGHT SIDE

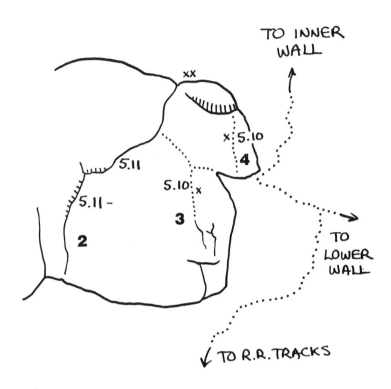

THE GARDEN WALL

The Garden Wall is located at the start of the Inner Wall trail, and is easily identified by both a long, curving crack in the center of the face, and a short, knobby wall on the upper right side. A path leads from the railroad tracks to this small cliff, and continues higher to the Inner Wall. It may also be approached from the Lower Wall.

1. **SHORT BUT DIRTY**   (−★★) **5.10+** (not shown)
    A short, trivial route on the extreme left side of the rock. Not worth it. FA: Darryl Cramer, 1982.

2. **A TOUCH TOO MUCH**   ★ **5.11b (R/X)**
    The obvious curving crack. Protection to 2″, and is difficult to place. Best toproped. FA: Darryl Cramer (almost).

3. **WEED-B-GONE**   **5.10c (R)**
    On the lower right side is this steep slab, with a single bolt protecting the most difficult section. Protection to 1″ FA: Mark Boatsman, 1982.

4. **KNOB JOB**   ★ **5.10d**
    This is the short knobby face on the upper right side of the wall, with a bolt and pin for protection. FA: Mark Boatsman 1982.

5. **TURKISH HEELS**   ★ **5.11a** (not shown)
    This route is on a small wall on the right (the K Cliff) as you approach the Inner Wall. This short route has a challenging crux start. Bring extra small nuts. A left leaning ramp (5.3) can be used to descend or to set up a top rope. FA: Terry Lien, Darryl Cramer, 1985.

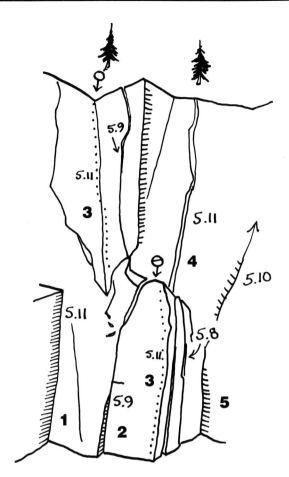

INNER TOWN WALL — LEFT SIDE

The Inner Town Wall is actually a narrow canyon between the Lower Wall mass and the Lower Lump on the left. Most of the routes are found at the highest point of the gap, although a few routes have been and will be done on the many walls on either side as one approaches this area. A trail leads left from the Lower Wall, meeting another path at the Garden Wall.

1. **VIEW FROM THE BRIDGE** ★ **5.11b (PG- 13)**
   This is the steep but short corner on the far left side which provides an interesting problem. Protection is difficult; try using RPs. FA: John Nelson, 1982.
2. **TOXIC SHOCK** ★★★ **5.9**
   An excellent steep handcrack on the left wall of a dihedral. The route starts with a short lieback, and may be divided into two pitches. Protection to 3". FA: Steve Strong 1981.
3. **SLAP SHOT** ★ **5.11d/5.12a**
   Climb the blunt arete right of the start of Toxic Shock to the pedestal, then cross Toxic Shock to the prow on the left of that route. Bolts. FA: Jim Yoder, Matt Kerns, 1988.

4. **EVEN STEVEN** ★ **5.11b (PG-13)**
This is the obvious pair of thin cracks on the overhanging wall just right of Toxic Shock. It begins with 5.8 twin cracks just right of the arete of Slap Shot. Protection to 1", including small wired and camming devices, as protection is difficult. FA: Dan Lepeska, Dick Cilley, 1982.

5. **FRED'S CORNER** **5.10b**
Just right of the twin crack start to Even Steven is this unusual dihedral with a crack. It was very overgrown prior to the first ascent. Protection to 2". FA: Fred Grafton, Jim Yoder 1988.

6. **TANG** ★ **5.11b/c** (not shown)
This is the thin crack and face on the left wall at the entrance to the large cave. Protection to 1". FFA: John Nelson, Terry Lien, 1984.

7. **FOODBAR** **5.11b** (not shown)
An overhanging thin crack about 60 feet right of the cave. Faced with tons of dirt and ferns, the first ascent party ended this climb rather abruptly; it could go on for several pitches. Protection to 1". FA: Darryl Cramer, John Nelson, Nicola Masciandaro, 1984.

8. **REPO MAN** **5.10a** (not shown)
This is a dark right-facing corner with a fixed pin, ending on a bushy ledge. It is about 30 yards right past the cave. Protection to 2". FA: Rick Graham, Brian Scott 1984.

9. **BEHIND THE EIGHT BALL** ★ **5.10a (PG- 13)** (not shown)
Farther along the left wall of the canyon is this off-width crack which passes a roof near its end. Tube chocks. FA: Kjell Swedin, Dick Cilley, 1981.

INNER WALL – RIGHT SIDE (not shown)

10. **DELUSIONS OF GRANDEUR** ★ **5.10c (PG-13)**
This steep face pitch is located on the right side of the canyon, across from the large cave. It passes a band of overhangs near the top. May be dirty. Protection to 1". FA: Steve Strong, 1981.

11. **AGENT ORANGE** **5.11a (R)**
Directly across the canyon from Toxic Shock, on the right side of the Grandeur buttress, is this defoliated slabby face climb. It is difficult to protect, and infrequently led. RPs are recommended. FA: Jeff Smoot, 1983.

12. **CORNER FLASH** ★ **5.7**
This is the obvious wide handcrack up a rounded buttress right of Agent Orange. Belay in the bushes. Protection to 3". FA: unknown.

13. **TRAP BALLS** ★ **5.10d**
In the narrow canyon right of Agent Orange is this short route. Start in a small cave and climb the overhanging crack to a ledge. Continue to the top of the short wall. Protection to 2". FA: Steve Strong, 1981.

14. **TOM'S TRAVERSE** **5.9**
From the ledge on Trap Balls, traverse right and climb a short crack to the top of the wall. Protection to 2". FA: Tom Michael, 1981.

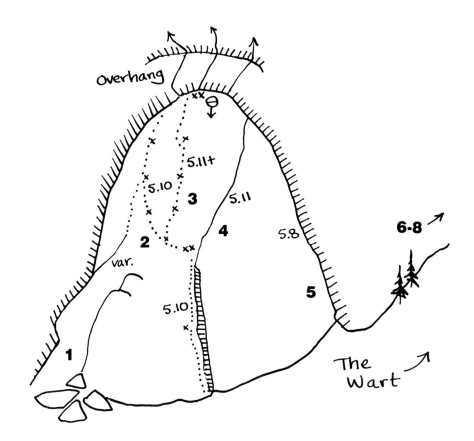

LOWER LUMP

The Lower Lump is the dark, blocky, forested dome on the far left side of the Lower Wall formation. The routes here are generally aid climbs, with blocky scrambling and short aid sections. There is little quality climbing here, and identifying the routes is not easy. With that in mind, good luck!

1. **CONFETTI   5.7 A2**
   On the left side of the Lump is an arch. Free climbing up slabs on the left leads to the overhangs, which are aided. Largely unknown. Numerous to 2", including a rurp. FA: Dave Anderson, John Teasdale.

2. **RACER 'X'   ★★ 5.10a/b**
   Climb the first pitch of Beetle Bailey . The second pitch traverses left and then up. If you do not traverse far enough left, you will be climbing Metal, not Racer 'X'. A #3 Friend is useful for a hole on the second pitch. Follow bolts to the top of slab. FA: Darryl Cramer, Terry Lien, 1986.

3. **METAL   ★ 5.11d**
   Climb the first pitch of Beetle Bailey. The route weaves a cramped line between Racer 'X' and Beetle Bailey. At the crux, a fixed pin is (currently) off route. Fixed protection. FA: Darryl Cramer, Terry Lien, Max Dufford 1986.

4. **BEETLE BAILEY** ★ **5.11a A3**
An obvious direct crack in a slab leads to overhangs. The first pitch takes a lieback up a flake from the base of the slab. Bolts and pins protect to the arch. Aid above slabs. Numerous to 2". FA: Donn Heller, Bruce Garrett, 1971; FFA: Terry Lien, Darryl Cramer, Brian Scott, 1986 (2 pitches).

5. **CONGOLINDINATION 5.8 A3**
This route climbs up a left-facing arch. Largely unknown. Numerous to 2". FA: Dave Anderson, Bruce Carson.

6. **CUPCAKE 5.10b/c** (not shown)
This route and Crispy Bacon begin atop The Wart, a small bump also known as the Lowest Lump. The first pitch climbs a left facing corner to a two bolt belay. The second traverses right to a finger crack (5.9). Protection unknown. FA: unknown.

7. **CRISPY BACON 5.10c (PG-13)** (not shown)
This route climbs the face left of the first pitch of Cupcake. Protection unknown. FA: unknown.

8. **WALKING BACK TO HAPPINESS 5.11d/12a (R)** (not shown)
Right of the Wart, climb face to arch, to roof and corners. Protection difficult; some bolts. FA: Greg Child, Greg Collum, 1988.

9. **SNOWDONIA 5.10c**
This route starts at a lone fir tree. Climb left across ledges into a gully/chimney. Largely unknown. FA: Donn Heller, John Waterman; FFA: Jim Yoder, 1987.

10. **BILLY'S CORNER 5.10c/d**
A crack/corner system just right of Snowdonia's chimney. Protection to 2"; should include stoppers, TCUs. FA: Matt Kerns, Jim Yoder, Bill Crawford 1987.

11. **SENTRY BOX** ★ **5.10a/b**
From the former fir tree, traverse left and climb a direct crack and corner into the "Sentry Box" roof. The original ascent party took a rightward exit; the free ascent went left. Protection to 3½". FA: Don Brooks; FFA: Jim Yoder, Matt Kerns, Bill Crawford 1987.

12. **FANG OVERHANG 5.10d**
The prominent overhang directly above the "tree". Protection to 4"; many small pieces. FA: Jim Yoder, Steve Gerberding 1988.

13. **NO HOBBY** ★ **5.11a/b**
A shallow corner system right of the Fang leads to a slabby face finish. Bolts, protection to 2½". FA: Matt Kerns, Jim Yoder 1988.

LOWER LUMP – RIGHT SIDE

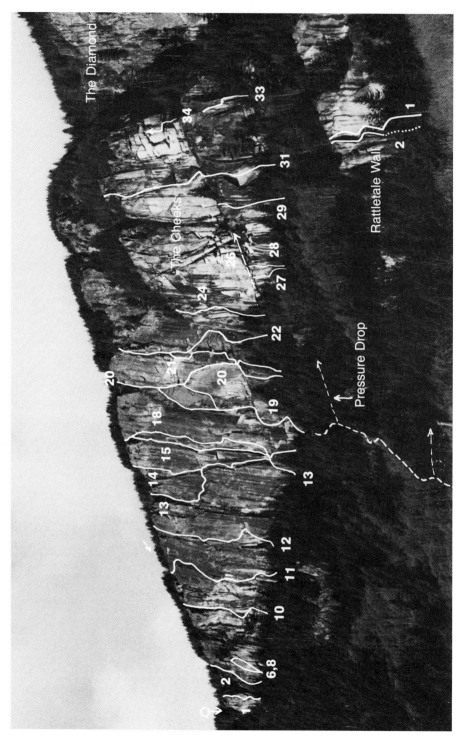

The Diamond

The Cheeks

Rattletale Wall

Pressure Drop

UPPER TOWN WALL

UPPER TOWN WALL

The Upper Town Wall is so obvious from town that it needs no real description. It is best to park either beside the tracks near the Bush House Inn, across the street from the same, or to walk along the tracks from the Lower Wall, leaving the car there.

The trail begins from the grassy road above the tracks, about 100 yards west of the mesh gate, passing a culvert. The track ascends steeply at places, crosses boulders at others, and leads one to the base of the wall, near **Pressure Drop**. A low path leads rightward toward **Zipper** and the Diamond, while a higher trail takes one along the base of the wall in either direction.

Incidental cliffs in this area include the extensive Lookout Point, a dome-like cluster of shorter cliffs below and right of the Upper Wall, as seen from town; Private Idaho, a short cliff band on the lower right, visible above the trees, and reached by a fine path starting just before the main trail, heading rightward along a shelf; and Rattletale, directly below the Zipper, and reached from either side trail with a bit of bushwhacking and luck.

Equipment needed for these routes varies, but one should be amply prepared for the "Big Wall Experience," especially on the longer and more serious routes, and should rack accordingly.

Descents are best made via a rappel route in place beside a gully left of **Backroad**, where one long or two shorter rappels from a tree gains the base of the cliff. It is also possible, although not highly recommended, to outflank the wall on the left side.

1. **SPORTFISHING** ★★ **5.10c**
   Left of a prominent gully on the left side of the Upper Town Wall is this three pitch route. The route takes a steep flake to a crack in a bubbly white wall, passing several ledges, to reach the top of the wall. Protection to 2". FA: Don Brooks, Dave Whitelaw, 1982.

2. **FRIENDS IN HOLY PLACES   5.10 A2 (?)**
   An "aid" route taking a line right of **Sportfishing**, on the right side of the gully. It may have been climbed free. Numerous to 2", including Friends. FA: Don Brooks, 1982.

3. **VANESSA DEL RIO   5.12d** (not shown)
   Face left of Everest Without Lycra. Bolts. FA: Greg Child, 1988.

4. **EVEREST WITHOUT LYCRA   5.11b/c** (not shown)
   Left arete of dirty corner left of **Domestic Violence**. Bolts. FA: Greg Child, Greg Collum, 1988.

5. **DARRYL'S DEMISE   5.11a** (not shown)
   Corner left of **Domestic Violence**. Protection unknown. FA: Darryl Cramer, 1988.

6. **DOMESTIC VIOLENCE** ★★ **5.11b**
   Right of **Sportfishing** are two crack lines which were once short aid routes. This is the left-most of them, taking the prominent straight crack. All three cracks pass through the overhangs to reach a ledge above. Protection to 2", with RPs. FA: Terry Lien, John Nelson, 1983.

7. **KILL SLUG   5.12a A0 (PG-13)** (not shown)
   This is the crack between **Domestic Violence** and **Earwax**. Protection to 2½", including TCUs and wired stoppers. FA: Greg Collum 1988.

8. **EARWAX (aka Gold Crack)** ★★★ **5.11b (PG-13)**
This is the thin crack up a gold wall just right of **Domestic Violence**. The beautiful thin crack slants noticeably to the right. One will need triplicate sets of RPs to protect this continuous line. FA: Don Harder, Dougal McCarty; FFA: Terry Lien, John Nelson, 1983.

9. **YOUNG CYNICS** ★ **5.12b A0** (not shown)
Bolted face right of Earwax. FA: Greg Collum 1988.

10. **BACKROAD** **5.8**
Right of the aforementioned cracks is this route (about 100 yards left of **Lamplighter**). The climb takes a series of flakes, corners, and face sections to a dirty chimney at the top. Protection to 2". FA: Jim Langdon, Pete Sandstedt 1968.

11. **DANA'S ARCH** ★ **III, 5.11 A3**
This obvious arch right of **Backroad** leads to a bolted face, and to "Cheeto Ledge." The arch has been bolted, and goes free at 5.11b. It should no longer be used for nailing practice. Aid on the bolts is easy. A3 nailing and bolts lead to easier climbing above Cheeto Ledge with a final short aid section at the top. Numerous to 3". FA: Bob Crawford, Leigh Nason, Pat Timson, 1970; FFA: Darryl Cramer, John Nelson, 1983 (Arch).

12. **LAMPLIGHTER** **IV, 5.8 A3**
Just right of Dana's Arch, climb the righthand chimney up to and over a roof (A3) to reach a belay at the base of a chimney. The remainder of the route is mostly free, taking chimneys of various widths, with intermittent aid sections. Numerous to 3", including KBs. The prominent off-width crack left of the first pitch is 5.10+. FA: Dave Dailey, Al Givler 1971.

13. **DAVIS-HOLLAND** ★★★ **III, 5.10c**
This route takes a hand crack to the broad ledges from which **Town Crier** and **Green Drag-On** also begin. The lefthand curving corner leads to a sling belay, and a short face pitch brings one to a comfortable ledge. It is best to either rappel (two 150-foot, with poor anchors), or climb **Lovin' Arms** to exit, avoiding the grungy upper chimney at all costs. It is also possible to rappel the route. Protection to 3". FA: Dan Davis, John Holland, 1964; FFA: Al Givler, Mead Hargis, Jay Ossiander, Pete Doorish.

14. **LOVIN' ARMS** ★★★ **IV, 5.10c A0 or 5.11c (R)**
From the third belay (the comfortable ledge) on Davis-Holland, go straight up the chimney to a bolt belay. Exit rightward onto the face, with very exposed climbing (one aid move from bolt, or a 5.11 move), or continue up the chimney and traverse higher up (easier), then continue to the top of the wall. Protection to 3". FA: Don Brooks, 1981; FFA: Pat Timson, 1984 (5.11 variation); Tom Hargis (free solo), 1986.

15. **THE GREEN DRAG-ON** ★ **IV, 5.11a A3**
Just down and right from the start of Davis-Holland, climb a thin crack pitch (5.11) to the ledge. Steep cracks and a long corner lead to the top. Numerous including many LAs, KBs, and hooks, to 3". FA: Don Harder, Donn Heller, 1973.

16. **NON-LOCAL BARK HOUSE** **5.11c** (not shown)
Lefthand of two diagonal cracks right of the start of **Green Dragon**. Protection unknown. FA: John Nelson, Greg Olson, Terry Lien, 1986.

17. **STEEL POLE BATHTUB** **5.11a** (not shown)
Righthand of two diagonal cracks just right of the start of **Green Dragon**. Protection unknown. FA: John Nelson, Terry Lien, Greg Olson, 1986.

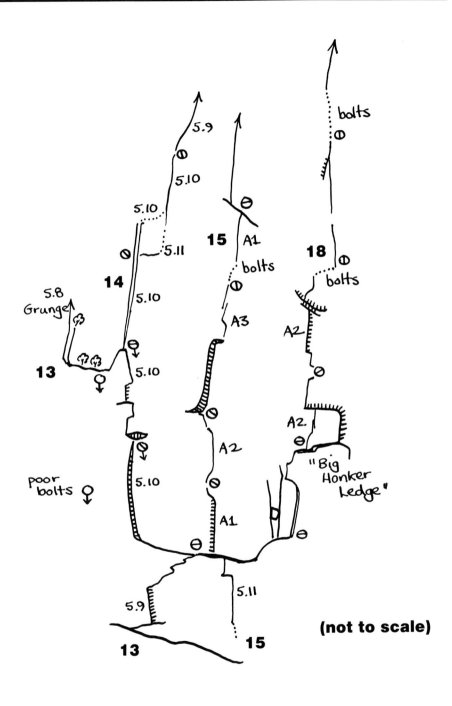

UPPER TOWN WALL – DAVIS-HOLLAND AREA

18. **THE TOWN CRIER** ★★★ **IV, 5.8 A2**
This route starts from the ledges mentioned previously. Climb a chimney rightward to "Big Honker Ledge," then take an arch through several tiered roofs, where aid leads to a long bolt ladder. Numerous to 3", including KBs and LAs. FA: Fred Beckey, Dave Beckstead, 1966.

19. **WATERWAY** ★★ **IV, 5.7 A3**
This route may be wet, as it takes the path of the "waterfall," and should not be climbed unless dry. A roof right of Town Crier may be passed via two variations on the extreme right side, to reach a ledge. Aid climbing leads to a narrow ledge, where the route splits, the right variation reaching the crack at the top of the arch on The Golden Arch (5.8 A2), while the left variant takes A3 to a tension traverse from a bolt, then aid cracks to join The Golden Arch. Numerous to 2", including KBs and LAs. FA: Les Davenport, Jim Stoddard, 1967.

20. **THE GOLDEN ARCH** ★★★ **IV, 5.11 A2+**
Three variation starts lead to Madsen's Ledge; the middle variation is the "proper" start. The left-hand route takes aid (A3); the middle route is 5.11b/c (FFA: Kjell Swedin, Eric Winkelman); the right-hand version is a 5.8 chimney pitch. A long aid pitch leads to the huge arch (A2+). Numerous to 3", including hooks and many LAs. FA: Jim Madsen, Ron Burgner 1967.

21. **ABRAXAS** ★★ **IV, 5.7 A4**
Any of the three variation starts leads to the ledge. Climb rightward from the start of The Golden Arch, past a stack of pillars, heading right under a flake to a sling belay beneath a roof. Hook moves above the roof are followed by easier aid to a sling belay above a higher overhang. An expanding flake leads to a short aid pitch at the top. Numerous to 3", including hooks, rurps, and bongs. FA: Pat Timson, Bob Crawford 1972.

22. **THE AVE** ★★ **IV, 5.8 A4**
From the top of the chimney variation start, traverse directly rightward to the base of several arches. Climb through the arches and the steep wall above (one pitch of A4, one of A3) to meet Abraxas at the top of the expanding flake. The route continues up corners and cracks, paralleling Abraxas on the right. Numerous to 3", including hooks, rurps, bongs, and mashies, mostly below 1". FA: Jim Langdon, Mark Weigelt 1969.

23. **ELECTROMATIC MARK IV** **5.12b** (not shown)
Thin layback flake left of start of Wilmon's Walk-About. FA: Max Dufford.

24. **WILMON'S WALK-ABOUT** **III, 5.11c A2**
Above Pressure Drop wall, right of the gully splitting the Cheeks and the Upper Wall proper, is this four pitch crack line. Pitches one, two and three are 5.11c, 5.10d, and 5.10c, respectively. The last pitch is A2. FFA: Terry Lien, Darryl Cramer, Max Dufford, 1987 (1st, 2nd, 3rd pitches).

25. **SEDAN DELIVERY** **5.11d** (not shown)
A crack up a knobby, concave wall beside second pitch of Wilmon's. FA: Terry Lien, Darryl Cramer, 1987.

26. **PERVERSE TRAVERSE** **(−★★) 5.6**
A horrible traverse which reaches the Prance Platform from the left side, via unprotected blocky climbing. Not recommended. FA: who cares?

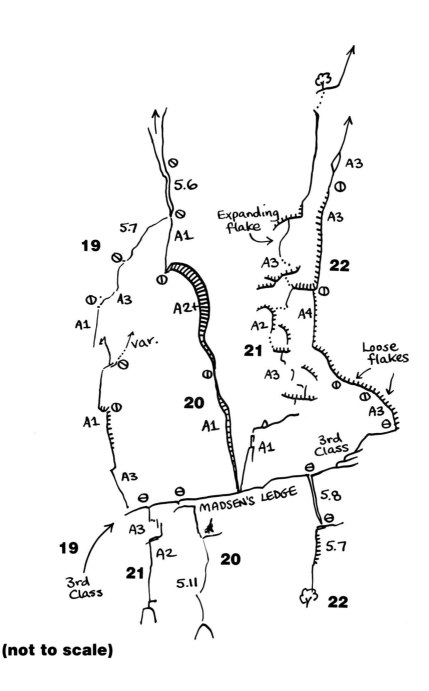

(not to scale)

UPPER TOWN WALL – GOLDEN ARCH AREA

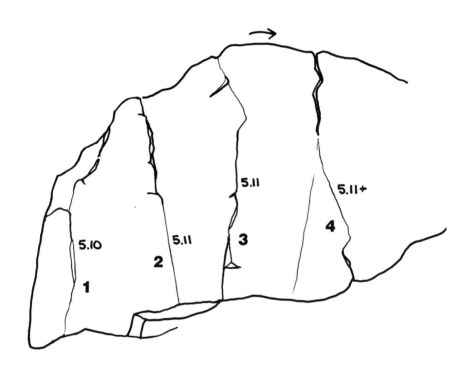

PRESSURE DROP WALL

The Pressure Drop Wall is the short cliff on the right at the end of the Upper Wall trail. Three of the four routes follow obvious thin cracks, the left-most being **Pressure Drop.**

1. **GREEN IS HERE   5.10c**
   Overgrown double thin cracks on the left side. Protection to 1". FA: Nicola Masciandaro, Darryl Cramer 1985.

2. **PRESSURE DROP   ★★ 5.11a**
   This is the straight-in finger crack on the left side of the short wall. Protection to 2". FA: Bob McDougall, Kjell Swedin, 1979.

3. **BLAME IT ON CAIN   5.11b (R)**
   A steep and very thin crack just right of Pressure Drop. FA: Dick Cilley, 1984; FLA: Max Dufford, 1988.

4. **ERROL FLYNN ON PIANO   5.11d (R)**
   Right of Blame it on Cain is this overhanging seam/lieback route. RPs, poor protection. FFA: Dick Cilley 1984 (TR); FLA: Max Dufford, 1987.

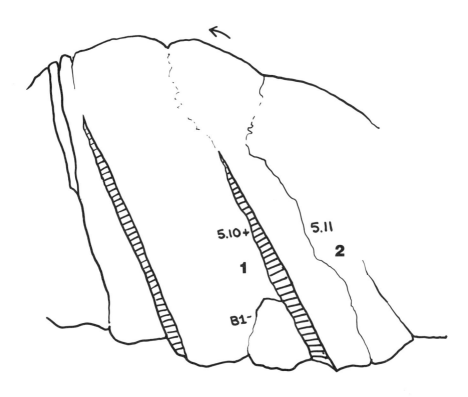

The following routes are located on a short wall reached by traversing rightward from the Pressure Drop wall.

1. **UNIVERSAL LANGUAGE (aka STAGE ONE) 5.12a (R)**
   An angular leaning corner on a slab, making for interesting face and stemming moves. A bouldering start leads to 5.10+ slab climbing. Protection uncertain, but sparse. FA: Dick Cilley, 1984 (TR); Kjell Swedin, Eric Winkelman, 1986.
2. **LET'S GO CRAZY 5.11+ (PG-13)**
   Just right of Universal Language is this very thin crack on the slab, which is best top-roped although it was initially led. RPs recommended. May need gardening. FA: Dick Cilley 1984.

UPPER WALL – ZIPPER AREA – THE CHEEKS

By continuing rightward from Pressure Drop wall, one passes beneath a steep, white streaked wall. Clay will be the first obvious route. The Zipper is also very obvious. By continuing right, one will reach the Diamond gully. The Cheeks formation is identified by deep gullys above Prance Platform.

27. **BLACK PLANET   5.9**
Below Perverse Traverse on shelf up and right from Let's Go Crazy, climb knobs past a bolt to a corner. FA: Darryl Cramer, Jeff Baird, 1986.

28. **HEAT SEEKER   5.11+ (TR)**
A thin flake on a steep wall right of Black Planet which is top-roped. This pitch ends on the Perverse Traverse. May need gardening. FA: Andy Cairns, 1984.

29. **CLAY   ★★★ 5.11d (PG-13)**
Climb a striking white open book, which overhangs in its entirety. This climb is located 150 feet left of Zipper, and is easily identified by the initial four inch crack. Protection to 3", with RPs recommended. Final slab (5.10+) leads to Prance Platform. FA: Terry Lien, John Nelson 1984.

30. **FICTION   5.11b (X) (not shown)**
In the Zipper amphitheatre, this is the left- hand slab. This bolt-protected line was initially top-roped. Very run out; groundfall from high up possible. FLA: Greg Child 1984.

31. **ZIPPER   ★★ IV, 5.10b A2**
The first pitch of this route is a popular corner and thin crack (5.10). The next pitch, the "Ice Cream Scoop" (roof), is nailed via either of two variations to reach Prance Platform. From that ledge, continue straight up thin cracks for two pitches of direct aid and some free climbing. Numerous to 4", including KBs. FA: Dennis Fenstermaker, Brent Hoffman, Karl Kaiyala, 1971 (Mark Weigelt climbed the first pitch in 1970).

32. **TANGO FOR TWO   5.10c (R) (not shown)**
This route climbs the right-hand corner of the amphitheatre, taking to the face when a line of knobs becomes apparent. Poor protection on slab. Protection to 4". FA: Dan Lepeska, 1982.

33. **LESS THAN ZERO   5.11b**
This is on the far right side of the wall, a steep chimney leading to a wildly curving arch. A rappel anchor is set up at the top of the arch. Protection to 3". FA: John Stoddard, 1980.

34. **LIEN-MICHAEL   5.11b**
An indirect line up and around roofs on the far right side of Prance Platform. Only one pitch has been completed so far; if a second pitch goes, the rating will be substantially increased. Protection unknown. FA: Terry Lien, Tom Michael, 1985.

Doug Weaver follows the Great Northern Slab, The Slab Area

THE DIAMOND – DIHEDRAL AREA

The Diamond is the broad, blank cliff to the right of the Upper Wall. A huge dihedral is its only striking feature. An incredibly gargantuan boulder lies at its base.

1. **THE DARK CRYSTAL**   ★★★ **5.11b**

   An excellent three pitch climb taking a wild arch and successive leaning corners just left of Dihedral to a ledge several hundred feet up. The first and final pitches are the most difficult. Protection to 3", with Friends recommended. FA: Cal Folsom, Kjell Swedin, 1984.

2. **DIHEDRAL**   **IV, 5.8 A4**

   The very obvious open book. The route starts behind the massive block, and is as straightforward as can be. From the dihedral's top, traverse rightward to easier but dirty climbing to reach the top. Descend eastward, or rappel Centerfold. Numerous to 2", with many below 1". FA: Dana Dudley, Jim Langdon, 1970.

3. **CENTERFOLD**   ★★★ **5.10d/11a (PG-13)**

   A spectacular route straight up the center of the Diamond. Begins about 50 yards right and uphill from Dihedral, in an obvious crack system. Route ends atop pillar. Rappel the route. Protection to 2"; take RPs, TCUs. Four pitches. FA: Cal Folsom, Andy Tuthill, 1988.

4. **HELL BENT FOR GLORY**   ★ **5.10d**

   This four-pitch route begins with a prominent dihedral right of the start of Centerfold. Go right at the horizontal break, then left from the cave. Rappel the route. Protection to 4", including double 2½" to 4". FA: Jim Yoder, Fred Grafton 1988.

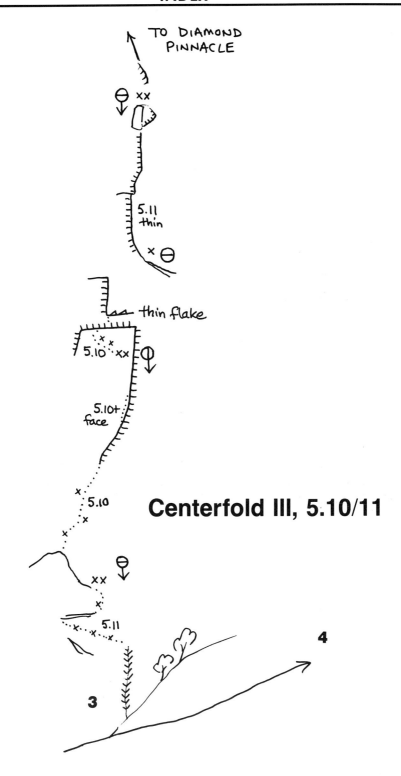

TO DIAMOND
PINNACLE

5.11
thin

thin flake

5.10

5.10+
face

5.10

Centerfold III, 5.10/11

5.11

4

3

RATTLETALE WALL

This is the lowest cliff band, located directly below the Zipper area of the Upper Town Wall, directly above the Bush House Inn. It is best approached either by traversing rightward from the initial talus slope on the Upper Wall trail, or by taking the left fork trail below Private Idaho.

1. **RATTLETALE** ★ **5.10a**

   A progression of dihedrals on the lowest visible wall, directly above the Bush House. The first pitch is dirty, but the second corner is excellent. Protection to 3", with Friends recommended. FA: Dave Anderson, Cal Folsom, Phil McCrudden 1979.

2. **NON-STOP EROTIC CABARET   5.11d (R)**

   Climb aretes left of Rattletale. Bolts, runouts. Protection: include a #5 Hexcentric and a 2½ Friend. FA: Greg Child, Greg Collum, 1987.

LOOKOUT POINT AREA

This is the group of cliffs located below and right of the Main Wall and Diamond areas, directly above the town of Index. A good trail starts near the Upper Wall trail (just past the gate at a "bridge" crossing the ditch), and winds upward. This trail ends at Private Idaho. One may scramble right or leftward from there. The ledge above that cliff provides a traversing approach to The Wall of 10,000 Insects.

THE WALL OF TEN-THOUSAND INSECTS

This small cliff is located at the base of the Diamond Gully, on the right. There are also a few routes along the right side of the gully as one ascends toward the Diamond.

1. **INDEX AIR FORCE** ★ **5.10b**

   Left of the obvious roof on 10,000 Insects Wall is this flake and thin crack leading to a short overhang. Protection to 2". FA: Cal Folsom, Don Brooks, 1983.

2. **THEM   5.10**

   Just right of Index Air Force is this obvious clean 4" crack and flake with a short overhang at the start. Protection to 4". FA: Cal Folsom, Don Brooks, 1983.

3. **SWEETS FOR MANUEL   5.10b (R)** (not shown)

   At the upper end of Diamond Gully is a clean dihedral system. Route ends in trees. Rope drag, loose rock near top. Protection to 2½". FA: Jeff Kelly, Matt Arksey 1987.

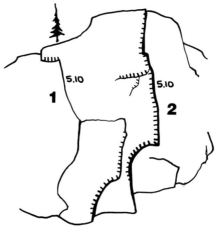

LOOKOUT POINT AREA

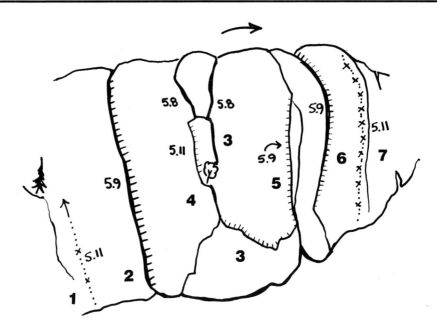

PRIVATE IDAHO

Private Idaho is the lowest band of cliffs on the right side of the Lookout Point area. There are a few routes on isolated cliffs on either side of this wall. An excellent trail reaches this cliff.

1. **ERASERHEAD   5.11c**
   A short bolted slab on the left side of the cliff, next to Wet Dream. FA: Greg Collum, Dan Cauthorn 1988.

2. **WET DREAM   ★ 5.9**
   The left-most route on the cliff, this is an obvious left-facing corner. Protection to 2". FA: Tish Nakaya and friend, 1984.

3. **MAGIC FERN   ★ 5.8**
   Right of Wet Dream is this off-hand crack pitch, leading to a ledge. A second pitch leads left from the ledge. Protection to 3". FA: Cal Folsom, Don Brooks 1984.

4. **CURIOUS POSE   ★ 5.11**
   A very short dihedral located between the previous routes, which provides a short crux. A maple tree grows at its base. A second pitch crosses Magic Fern at the ledge, ascending a short crack. Both of these can be done as one longer pitch. Protection to 2". FA: Cal Folsom, Dave Anderson, Don Brooks, 1984.

5. **ISTANBUL   5.9**
   Right of the previous routes is this hand and off-hand crack in a considerably right-leaning corner. Protection to 3". FA: Cal Folsom, Don Brooks, 1984.

6. **BATTERED SANDWICH   ★ 5.9**
   An obvious wild flaring crack right of Istanbul, on the far right side of this cliff. Protection to 4". FA: Ed Gibson, Steve Barnett, 1970; FFA: Lindi McIlwaine, Gale Nelson, 1984.

7. **SPINELESS   ★ 5.11b**
   The blunt buttress right of Battered Sandwich, with ten bolts. FA: Greg Collum, Greg Olsen 1988.

Bolt ladder start to City Park, Lower Town Wall

HAG CRAG (not shown)

Just right of Private Idaho is this small cliff with a large dihedral/chimney in the center. There are a few easier climbs on the right side.

1. **END GAME   5.9**
   An obvious, bolted slab on the left side. Looks harder than it is. Start 20 feet up a trough and traverse to bolt. FA: Don Brooks, Chris Syrjala, 1984.
2. **CRACK   5.10 (TR)**
   Traverse knobby face (crux) into wide slab crack. FA: unknown.
3. **VORTEX   5.7?**
   The dihedral/chimney system in the center of the slab. Protection unknown. FA: unknown.

LOOKOUT POINT

The following routes are located on the Lookout Point formation proper, which is the uppermost cliff band below the Diamond.

1. **STEEL PULSE   ★★ 5.10d (R/X)**
   On the right margin of the formation is this 3-pitch slab route. Start in an obvious clean gully/corner system. The first and second pitches are varied and enjoyable (may be broken into three pitches). There is a substantial easy runout on the second pitch; otherwise, the route is well protected. The final pitch passes two short overhangs and ends in trees. Rappel down the gully to Law and Order rappel or rappel into righthand gully. With a bolt anchor at the end of the "second" pitch, two clean rappels could be made down the route, eliminating the need to climb the third short pitch and the awkward descent. Protection to 1". FA: Jeff Kelly, 1983; FFA: Jeff Kelly, Jeff Boucher, Matt Arksey, 1987.
2. **SCRATCH AND CLAW   ★ 5.10b/c**
   Variation start to Steel Pulse up short dihedral and face traverse located 15 feet right of original start. Protection to ½", bolts. FA: Jeff Boucher, Jeff Kelly, 1987.
3. **LAW AND ORDER   ★★ 5.10c or 5.11a (R)**
   An obvious, long route up the middle right side of the formation, visible from town as a white streak. Starts with a shallow corner. Crux on second pitch. Several variations. Protection to 2"; 165-foot rope. Rappel the route. FA: Jeff Kelly, Matt Arksey, 1986; FLA: Kelly, Arksey.
4. **RICE KRISPIES   5.10**
   Left from Law and Order about 100 feet a corner/flake leads to a rappel anchor. A short pitch. Protection to 2". FA: John Nelson, Mark McKillip, 1982.
5. **BOBCAT CRINGE   5.12 A1**
   A striking, overhanging thin crack. FA: unknown.
6. **PURPLE KOOL-AID   5.10c**
   This route takes an arching flake to a dihedral. Take the approach pitch for Bobcat Cringe to this long, left-slanting corner. May be brushy. Protection to 2". FA: John Nelson, Greg Olsen.
7. **PEANUTS TO SERVE YOU   5.9**
   Climb thin flake to dihedral, which leads to bolt anchor shared with Purple Kool-Aid. Protection to 3". FA: Greg Olsen, John Nelson, 1981.
8. **BOWLING FOR BISCUITS   5.10d**
   On the far left side of the cliff is a short corner and crack system leading through an overhang to a belay below a prominent roof. The route continues up past the right side of the roof (crux there). Protection to 3". FA: John Nelson, Dave Toler, 1981.

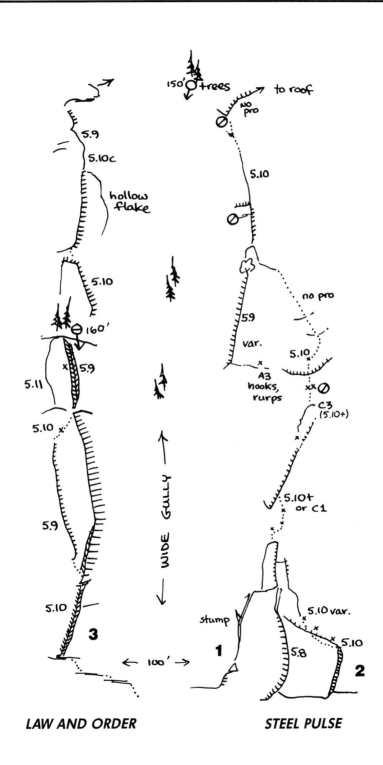

LAW AND ORDER

STEEL PULSE

ZAPPA WALL (not shown)

This short cliff is located very low down and right of Lookout Point, just above the town. It is identifiable by a band of short overhangs on a white wall just above the treetops.

1. **HOT CURLY WEENIE   5.10+ (R)**
   A curving crack with a dangerous flake at the start. Best top-roped. Protection unknown. FA: unknown.
2. **POOP CHUTE   5.8**
   This is a gross gully/chimney. Protection unknown. FA: unknown.
3. **SUCK ME IN, PLEASE   5.12a**
   Don't ask. Protection unknown. FA: Jim Yoder.

ZEKE'S WALL (not shown)

Across the railroad tracks from Zeke's Drive Inn, a favorite hamburger stand located between Startup and Index, are several obvious large granite walls. The rightmost cliff band has been climbed. With better access, this would be an area to rival the Lower Wall.

Take Reiter Road from Startup about one or two miles to the obvious left fork. Follow as far as you can, then hike a logging spur towards the base of the cliffs.

This area has much potential, but with the difficult approach, it is not popular.

STEVENS PASS - RAMONE ROCK

Located just north of the Stevens Pass Summit is this gem, a small weathered granite cliff with numerous cracks and an obvious small overhang. A dirt road heading north from the summit parking lot, passing several cabins, leads past a microwave relay station to a trail which passes above the cliff. The routes may all be led, with Friends advised for protection, although top-roping may be best. Routes are listed from left to right. All first ascents by Jeff Kelly, Chris Gentry, Kirk Johnson unless otherwise noted.

1. **SIDEWINDER   5.4**
   A wide crack with a chockstone on the far left side.
2. **SHEENA IS A PUNK ROCKER   5.8 or 5.9**
   The off-width crack opposite Sidewinder.
3. **TROGLODYTE IN FREE-FLIGHT   ★ 5.9**
   A curving crack just right of Sheena. 5.10 if you can eliminate Sheena. Protection to 1".
4. **SON OF A PITCH   ★ 5.10b**
   Another curving crack. Protection to 1½".
5. **VOID   5.8**
   A crack left of the chimney corner. Protection to 2".
6. **BRUISE ON THE BACK   5.7**
   Chimney in the corner. Protection to 3".
7. **GENTRY'S FACE   5.10 (TR)**
   A short face climb up prow of pillar.
8. **TEENAGE LOBOTOMY   ★★ 5.11a**
   A crack taking the left exit from beneath the overhang. Protection to 1". FA: John Stoddard (TR); FLA: Kelly.
9. **CRACK IN A HARD THIN ROOF   A1**
   A short aid crack in the roof.
10. **OBSCURA   5.10b**
    A short face climb, reached by a short traverse from the right. Protection to 1".
11. **PROCTOLOGY   5.8**
    A dirty corner crack. Protection to 2".
12. **A LUST FOR DUST   5.5**
    Just right of Proctology. Protection to 2".
13. **THANK GOD FOR BIG JUGS   5.8**
    A corner crack right of Lust For Dust. Protection to 2".
14. **TERRORIZER   5.9 (R)**
    Face climb right of Big Jugs. No protection. FA: Jeff Smoot (solo) 1988.
15. **MOUNTAINEER'S ROUTE   5.2**
    An easy scramble up a series of ramps and short faces on the right-hand side of the cliff. Starts with a short flake. Protection to 1".
16. **TROUBLE MAKER   5.0**
    An easier scramble right of the Mountaineer's Route, up ledges to a fun, short buttress. Protection to 1". FA: Jeff Smoot, Andrea Busch 1988.

RAMONE ROCK

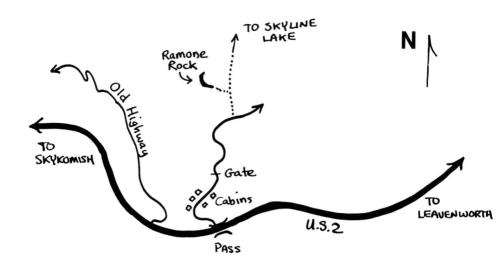

SKI AREA

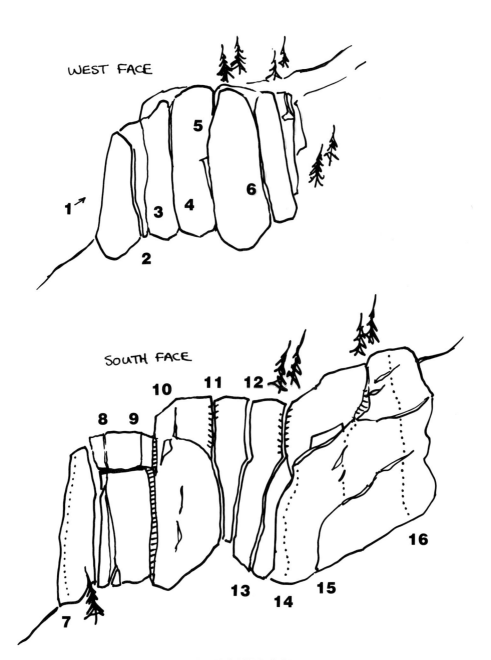

WEST FACE

SOUTH FACE

RAMONE ROCK

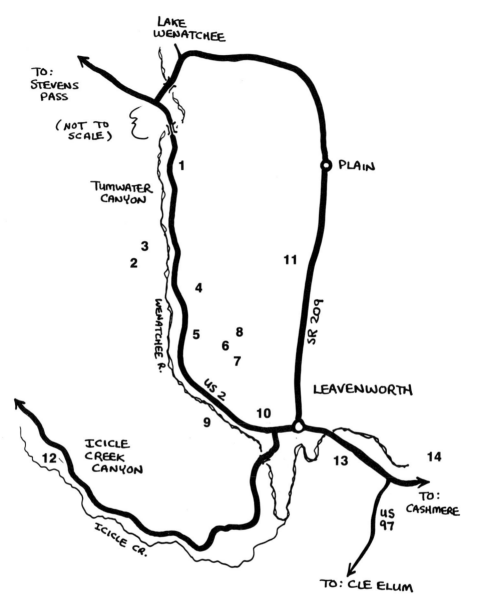

LEAVENWORTH AREA

1. Swiftwater
2. Waterfall Column
3. Jupiter Rock
4. Rattlesnake Rock
5. Castle Rock
6. Midnight Rock
7. Noontime Rock
8. Punk Rock
9. Tumwater Tower
10. Every Inch is Hard
11. Chumstick Snag
12. Snow Creek Parking Lot
13. Sandy Slab
14. Peshastin Pinnacles

LEAVENWORTH

Leavenworth, Washington, the "Bavarian Village," is without a doubt the hub of Washington rock climbing. This is mostly due to the fact that the town itself, not only the rock, provides a convenient place for climbers to meet. It is blatantly and unashamedly a tourist town, with Bavarian-style facades livening up an otherwise dull village on the east flank of the Cascades. However, without the rocks, Leavenworth would be the last place any self-respecting climber would want to go.

Leavenworth is located about 120 miles east of Seattle/Everett on U.S. 2. It may also be reached via I-90 and U.S. 7, a longer and less-direct approach from Puget Sound. There are four major climbing areas within 15 minutes' drive of town — Tumwater Canyon, Icicle Creek Canyon, Snow Creek Wall and Peshastin Pinnacles.

Tumwater Canyon, located just outside of town and reached via U.S. 2, is the most popular Leavenworth climbing area, largely because of Castle Rock, the most popular crag in the state. Midnight Rock is also a favorite, but farther from the road and less-frequently visited. Minor crags such as Rattlesnake Rock, Piton Tower and Tumwater Tower are also found here, along with the remote big walls of Jupiter Rock and Waterfall Column. Ice climbing in the winter is popular here as well, provided that the falls freeze solid. Drury Falls and the elusive Pencil are the best-known waterfall routes.

Icicle Creek Canyon, just southeast of town, is reached via the Icicle River Road. This canyon has much potential for new routes, even though it has been climbed in for the past 40 years. There are several campgrounds in the Icicle. Nightly fees are charged in most. Private property abounds, so be aware that you may be trespassing whenever you leave the road. If you are asked to leave, please do so. Don't camp alongside the road unless you know it is allowed.

The Snow Creek Wall, the largest of Leavenworth's crags, visible as you drive into Icicle Creek Canyon, is reached via a two-mile hike. The climbs here are long and airy, ranging from moderate classics to runout desperates. Some of the modern routes offer relentless 5.11 slab climbing high off the ground. Outer Space, the classic route on the wall, is seven pitches long, as are many of the routes here. Camping is available at the base of the wall, but bring your own water.

Peshastin Pinnacles, located just west of Cashmere on U.S. 2, is the only major climbing area in Washington that is not granitic. The rock here is Swauk sandstone, offering some of the best friction climbing in the state. Unfortunately, climbing here is now banned. Originally, the area was closed by the owner of the adjoining orchards each autumn during the apple harvest. Then, as it became a problem, parking was restricted to the right side of the road a quarter mile from the entrance only. Finally, in 1986, the area was permanently closed. The owner, apparently concerned about rising insurance premiums, felt the risk was not worth the cost – even though there has never been a climbing-related death at the Pinnacles (or a death by any other cause, either, as far as anyone knows). Efforts to buy the climbing area have failed. Until something is done, the area will remain closed. It is a sad loss, but hopefully not permanent.

The town of Leavenworth offers grocery stores, hotels and motels, showers, bars, restaurants, and a golf course for those so inclined (miniature golf, too). All too frequently, however, the town is crowded with tourists. There is Mai Fest, October Fest, and every other kind of fest, ensuring that the motel rooms and county coffers will be full. On such weekends, the campgrounds will probably be full, too.

The weather in Leavenworth is usually good – too good. In the summer, temperatures regularly reach 90 degrees and above. The locals claim 300 days of sunshine a year, making Leavenworth a good bet if it is raining in Seattle. The area is protected by a rainshadow from the Stuart Range, which cleaves off clouds to the south, leaving Leavenworth dry – usually. When raining in Leavenworth, climbers used to head for Peshastin. Now they just go to Gustav's Tavern and drink beer, or turn around and go home.

Climbers in Leavenworth should be wary of rattlesnakes in the summer and fall, and of ticks in the spring. Giardia is a major health problem, so don't drink stream water unless it has been boiled or otherwise sterilized. Eightmile and Bridge Creek Campgrounds both have wells with cold, clean water, as does the town.

PESHASTIN PINNACLES

The Peshastin Pinnacles are the light sandstone slabs and spires located just west of Cashmere along U.S. 2. The Pinnacles stand out from otherwise rolling hillsides, and comprise the only major climbing area in Washington that is not volcanic in origin.

Unfortunately, the Pinnacles are located on private property, a fact that is all too obvious in that the area has been closed to climbing since 1986. The landowner, who owns the adjoining apple orchards, closed the Pinnacles to climbing apparently to save money on his liability insurance. Until then, he had regularly closed the area each autumn during the apple harvest. Climbers have trespassed since, and there have been arrests. Efforts to buy the Pinnacles have so far failed. Hopefully, the area will not remain closed for long. However, in the meantime, don't climb there. The descriptions that follow are included both for the historical record and also in the faint hope that the area will be reopened with time.

The name is a misnomer – the Pinnacles are actually closer to Cashmere than Peshastin (Cashmere Crags was already taken). Drive east about 15 miles from Leavenworth (about 10 miles from Wenatchee) and turn up the first road on the north once you see the formations. Parking is allowed only along the right side where the road curves west. Make sure your car is parked off the concrete – otherwise, you may be ticketed or towed. When the area is packed, some park along the highway or in the orchards. This may not, however, be legal.

The rocks are approached via an access road through the orchards. Don't play in the orchards or pick fruit, or the area may be closed again. Be respectful of the owner's rights and of his orchards.

Climber-initiated erosion is a serious problem at the Pinnacles. Whenever possible, stay on the defined trails, and away from the base of the slabs. If you need proof that erosion is a problem, look at the base of Austrian Slab. When the dirt starts piling up in the orchards, the area may again be closed. Conservation efforts have so far not been organized, but are much needed.

Climbers at the Pinnacles – if they are ever allowed to climb there again – should beware that the bolts are not always good. Since the rock is soft, it erodes easily, especially around bolts. Many of the bolts placed in the 1950s and 1960s are still in use. How reliable is a 20-year-old 1/4-inch bolt placed in decomposing sandstone? Not very. If the area is reopened, be especially careful. Because climbers have not been doing the routes, the condition of the bolts and fixed pins will not be known – until somebody replaces or breaks them. Also, hammers should not be carried in the Pinnacles except to place or replace bolts and fixed pins. Repeated nailing and chipping have already damaged the rock enough.

Opinion was mixed as to whether Peshastin Pinnacles should be included in this guide. "The area is closed," one climber said. "Why bother?" Why? Frankly, because although the crags are closed, we shouldn't give up. They may be reopened someday if we keep some hope, and maintain some sense of right to climb there, however remote. If we simply say, "They're closed, don't bother," we certainly won't ever climb there again. The Pinnacles have a long history, and have been a favorite climbing area in the past. Hopefully, by including them in this guide, we will not forget about the Peshastin Pinnacles and abandon them as some apparently would have us do.

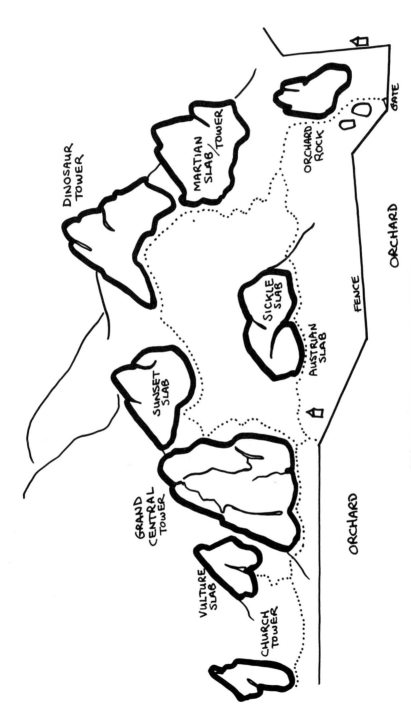

PESHASTIN PINNACLES OVERVIEW

DINOSAUR TOWER

MARTIAN SLAB / TOWER

ORCHARD ROCK

GATE

SICKLE SLAB

AUSTRIAN SLAB

FENCE

ORCHARD

SUNSET SLAB

GRAND CENTRAL TOWER

VULTURE SLAB

CHURCH TOWER

ORCHARD

ORCHARD ROCK

Orchard Rock is the squat pinnacle just inside the east entrance gate. Most routes lead to the higher summit, where an 80-foot rappel is used for descent. Bolts are in place on both summits for toproping or rappelling. The routes are listed from right to left.

1. **SCRAMBLE   5.0 (X)**
   Start on west face, down low near a tree, climb a ramp/groove, then traverse left on shelf and chimney to crux mantle onto summit. Protection imaginary. FA: unknown.

2. **CUNT CRACK   5.9+**
   Wide, overhanging crack above shelf (The Womb), right of chimney. Very obvious. Protection to 2". FA: unknown.

3. **OVERHANG   5.8+**
   Left of Scramble is this obvious overhang. The crux is higher up. Somewhat decomposing rock. Protection to 2". FA: unknown. Variation climbs face left of overhang, with several bolts in place. Rating unknown (5.10 or harder). FA: unknown.

4. **TUNNEL   ★ 5.6**
   From the notch, climb up through tunnel to a steep crack to summit. Protection to 2½". FA: unknown.

5. **GULLY   5.1**
   Wide crack/chimney on east face which leads to the upper notch. Protection to 1". FA: unknown.

6. **A CRACK   ★ 5.7**
   Short, overhanging hand crack just left of Gully. Direct variation is harder and somewhat rotten (ignore the bolt on the left). Protection to 2". FA: unknown.

7. **THE KNOBS   ★ 5.9**
   Climb sandy face down from the Gully via knobs, then rotten cracks to top. Not as bad as it sounds if bolts have hangers. Protection to 2". FA: unknown.

8. **THE TUBES (aka TUBAL LIGATION)   ★ 5.11a (X)**
   Wide, parallel "cracks" left of The Knobs with wild face finish to prow. Best toproped. FA: Jim Yoder (TR); FLA: Yoder, 1982.

9. **CORNER   5.2**
   Short corner left of Knobs leading to shelf below Cunt Crack. Protection to 1". FA: unknown.

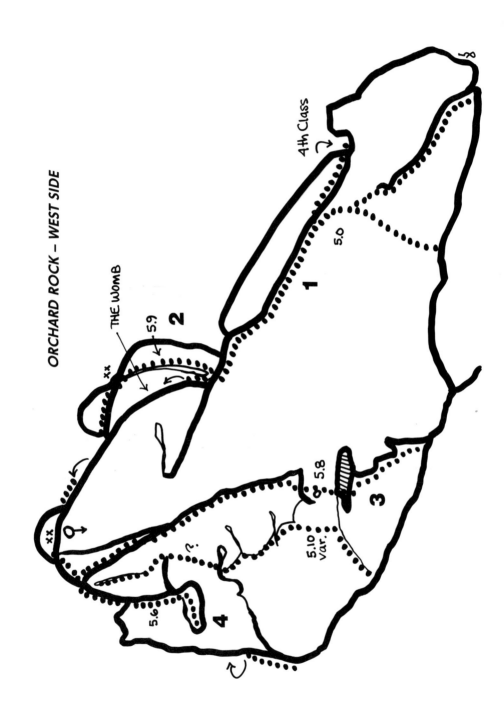

ORCHARD ROCK – WEST SIDE

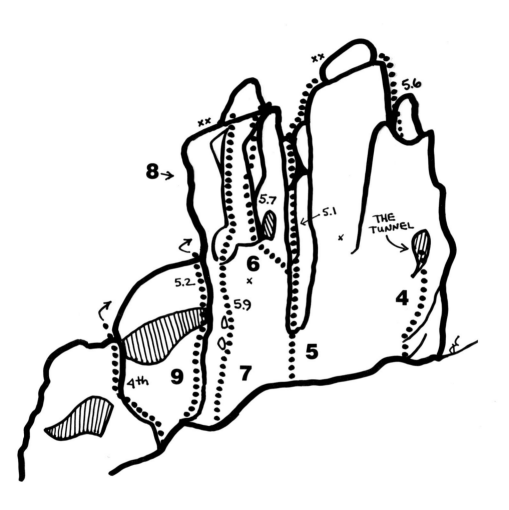

ORCHARD ROCK – EAST SIDE

MARTIAN SLAB/TOWER

Just uphill from Orchard Rock is the Martian Tower/Slab formation. The tower has a few routes which climb to or towards its summit, while the slab has several more routes criss-crossing it. Most routes are bolted. Descents are by rappel, either from near the summit of the tower or from the uppermost notch of the slab (the latter involving a 10-foot rappel or 5.7 downclimb). The routes are listed from right to left.

MARTIAN TOWER

1. **CATACOMBS   5.7**
   This route is directly above Orchard Rock, on the right side of the ridge. A short face crux into an odd chimney leads to the summit of the tower. Protection to 2". FA: Dan Davis, Dick Springgate, Dave Beckstead, Errin Duncan.

2. **GRAHAM CRACKER   5.10c**
   A short, bolt-protected variation start left of Catacombs. FA: Rick Graham, Brian Scott, 1980.

3. **BUTTER BRICKLE   5.8+**
   From the ridge crest, left of Graham Cracker, climb left and up wide, overhanging crack just left of the prow. Protection to 4". FA: Dave Becksted, J. Brottem, 1967; FFA: Bill Sumner.

4. **FROSTBACK FOLLIES   5.10a**
   A sandy route climbing through roof just left of Butter Brickle. Protection to 2". FA: unknown.

5. **WEST FACE   5.8**
   A diagonaling route from the slab on the left near the gap, reaching the summit directly. Protection to 2". FA: Fred Beckey, Eric Bjørnstad.

6. **SPIRAL   5.6** (not shown)
   A variation which supposedly climbs in circles around the tower before summitting. Protection unknown. FA: unknown.

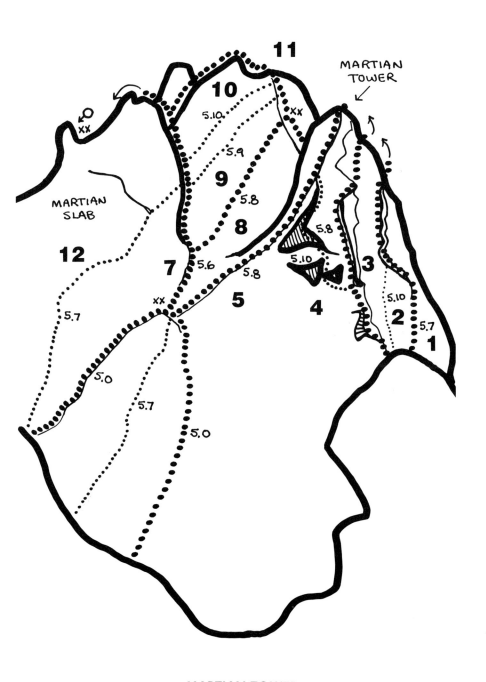

MARTIAN TOWER

MARTIAN SLAB

7. **DIAGONAL** ★★ **5.5 or 5.6**
Start from trees along base of slab. Several variation starts lead to a belay dish in the middle of the slab (leftmost variation is easiest). The second pitch leads leftward up friction to the obvious ramp. Fixed protection. FA: Dave Beckstead, Fred Stanley.

8. **DIAGONAL DIRECT** ★ **5.8**
From above the crux of Diagonal, traverse rightward to bolt-protected grooves and up. Fixed protection; old bolts. FA: Pat Callis, Dick McGowan.

9. **KIBBLES 'N BITS** **5.9 (R)**
Left of Direct is this poorly protected friction pitch. Fixed protection. FA: Mike Jakubal, 1983.

10. **EAT IT** **5.10b (R)**
Left of Kibbles 'n Bits is this equally poorly protected climb. Fixed protection. FA: Jim Yoder, 1983.

11. **RIDGE** **5.6**
From the notch of the tower, this route climbs the crest of Martian Slab, downclimbing at the end to connect with Diagonal. The preceding three routes connect with the Ridge. Protection to 2". FA: Fred Beckey.

12. **SERPENT** ★ **5.7 (R)**
Left of the leftmost variation start of Diagonal is this friction climb. Aim for the first bolt, then look for the rest. Somewhat run out. Connect with Diagonal, or traverse leftward to finish. Fixed protection. FA: Ed Vervoort, 1980.

13. **VOYAGER ONE** ★ **5.6**
Climb slab with bolts right of noticeable small cave. 165-foot rope. FA: Ed Vervoort, 1980.

14. **VOYAGER TWO** **5.7**
Move left from the aforementioned cave and up slab. Bolts. 165-foot rope. FA: Ed Vervoort, 1980.

15. **PORPOISE** **5.6**
Dihedral at upper left end of slab. Face climb on right and up potholes to top. Protection to 1". FA: unknown.

16. **HARPOON** ★ **5.10b**
Friction pitch squeezed in between Grey Whale and Porpoise. Fixed protection. FA: Jim Yoder, 1982.

17. **GREY WHALE** ★★ **5.8**
Friction pitch in center of wide grey slab at upper end of Martian formation. Bolts. FA: Bill Sumner, Al Givler.

18. **TORTOISE** **5.9**
Short route left of Grey Whale. Two bolts. Rotten rock at end. FA: Geoff Scherer, 1984. Variation: Friction right from first bolt (5.11?). FA: Jim Yoder, 1984.

19. **HUMPBACK WHALE** **5.8**
Short route right of Tortoise. Shares second bolt. Both this and Tortoise end at the Grey Whale belay. FA: Geoff Scherer, 1984.

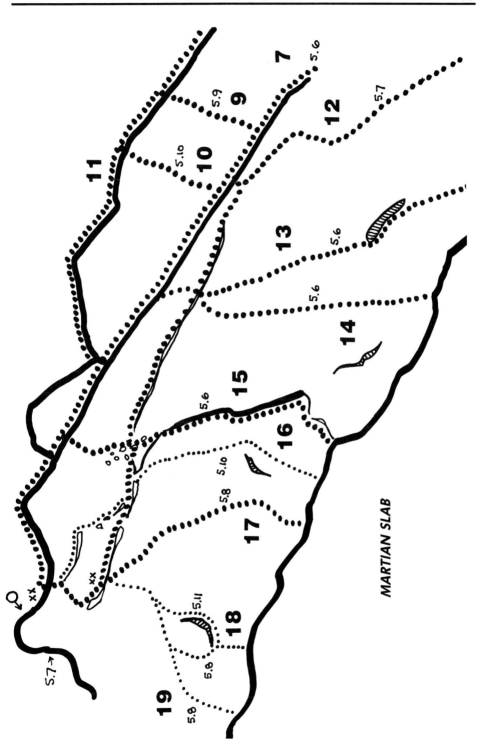

DINOSAUR TOWER

Dinosaur Tower is the big blob of sandstone perched atop the ridge above Martian Slab. It has several of the best friction routes in the area. Descents from the summit can be made by rappelling down the back side, then traversing a ledge and making a ten-foot rappel to the notch, or by rappelling 120 feet from the summit down the west face. The routes are listed from right to left.

1. **STONE AGE MAN** ★ **5.10** (not shown)
   Unique route climbing into cave at "nose" of formation, then out. Beware of owls nesting in cave. Bolts. FA: George Rohrbach, Jim Springer, Jim Yoder, 1985.

2. **SKYLINE** ★ **5.5**
   Climb crack on right then up ridge to rappel station at notch. This route has a very large chopped hold. Protection to 2". FA: Fred Beckey, Dick Widrig.

3. **OUT OF REACH** **5.10b-5.10d** (not shown)
   Variable difficulty depending on your reach. Climbs up groove, traverses left and passes overhang. Bear right to dihedral finish. Protection to 2½". FA: Rick LeDuc, 1981.

4. **POTHOLES** ★ **5.7 +**
   A Peshastin semi-classic starting with a leftward, follow-the-bolts face to a semi-hanging belay. The crux climbs over a steep wall on the left, and up cracks and chimneys above. Fixed protection. FA: Fred Beckey, Henry Mather, Don Gordon; FFA: Fred Beckey, E. Cooper.

5. **POTHOLES DIRECT** **5.10c (PG-13)**
   A direct variation to the first pitch, going up slab from lone tree and right from bulge. Fixed protection, but bring along a small Friend and camming units for pockets. FA: unknown.

6. **POTHOLES DIRECT DIRECT** ★★ **5.10a**
   From tree directly below Potholes belay, climb up slab and left from bulge into short corner (crux). Continue directly up face to join Potholes. Fixed protection. FA: Jim Langdon, Larry Richter, 1969.

7. **WASHBOARD** ★★★ **5.10b/c**
   From the aforementioned tree, climb left up rotten flakes to the interesting namesake slab, then traverse right to finish at the Potholes belay or undercling left to connect with Primate. Fixed protection. FA: Pat Timson, 1971.

8. **PRIMATE** ★ **5.10d**
   Climb slab left of Washboard (5.9, runout), to a thin crack in a corner. Traverse right to the Potholes belay. Bolts. FA: Fred Beckey, Dan Gordon, 1960; FFA: Jim Madsen.

9. **PRIMATE DIRECT** ★★ **5.11a (R/X)**
   A direct link between Washboard and Primate, traversing left to meet Primate at the start of its difficulties. Climb above last bolt of Washboard (fixed pin said to be missing), then move left and mantle into a corner. Fixed protection. A long fall onto old bolts is possible from the crux if the pin is gone. FLA: Jim Yoder, Lee Cunningham, 1986.

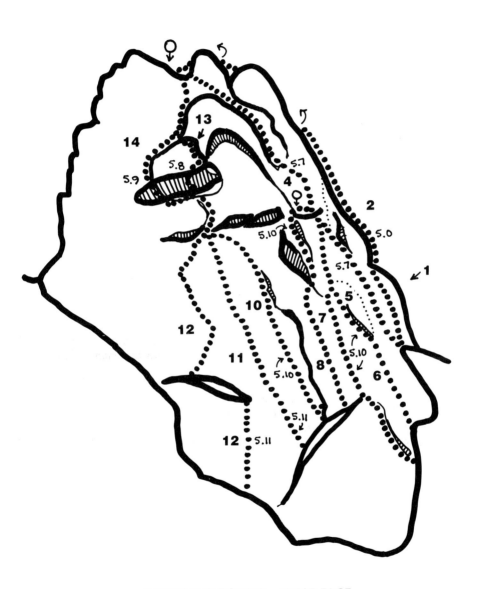

DINOSAUR TOWER – WEST FACE

10. **PEBBLES & BAM-BAM** ★★ **5.10b**
    Start at rotten flake left of Primate (original Primate start), and climb slab and flakes leftward to the Cro-Magnon belay ledge. Bolts. FA: Jim Yoder, Lee Cunningham, 1984.

11. **DR. LEAKEY** ★★★ **5.11b**
    From ledge left of Pebbles, climb difficult bulge and slab to Cro-Magnon belay. Bolts. FA: Rick LeDuc, Jamie Christensen (upper slab); Bob McGowan (direct start). Note: The original ascent party (upper slab) carved a hold, which can – and should – be avoided (it is only 5.11).

12. **IGUANADON** **5.11**
    Short friction pitch left of Dr. Leakey, with two bolts. Decomposed rock. FA: Jim Yoder, Bob Vaughan, 1986.

13. **CRO-MAGNON** **5.8**
    From ledges on far left side climb to belay beneath overhangs, then climb crack up and right through overhangs to the top. Double ropes helpful to eliminate rope drag. Protection to 2". FA: Dan Davis, P. Callis. Variation: Barney Rubble. Rating unknown. Supposedly a roof variation. FA: Rick LeDuc.

14. **CAVEMAN** **5.9+**
    From left edge of the aforementioned belay ledge, climb out roof. Protection to 2". FA: Fred Beckey, Frank Tarver, Herb Staley, 1959; FFA: unknown.

15. **PILTDOWN**   (–★) **5.7** (not shown)
    From notch, a short boulder problem gains a big ledge. Continue up and left, around to rappel anchors. Chipped holds. Not worthwhile. Protection to 2". FA: Fred Beckey and party. FFA: Dan Davis, Pat Callis. Variation goes right from ledge and up prow (5.9). FA: Dan Davis, Pat Callis.

16. **MISSING LINK**   (–★★) **5.8** (not shown)
    Start up rotten ramps below notch to reach "flaky trough." Not pleasant. Protection unknown – tied off, bent bolts? FA: Eric Bjørnstad, Henry Mather.

17. **MICKEY MOUSE CRACK**   (–★★) **5.8** (not shown)
    A short crack farther down from notch that has a lot of poor rock on the approach. Protection to 3". FA: unknown.

18. **HOLE IN THE WALL**   (–★★) **5.6** (not shown)
    Halfway up Mickey Mouse, traverse left. Useless route. Protection unknown. FA: Ed Vervoort.

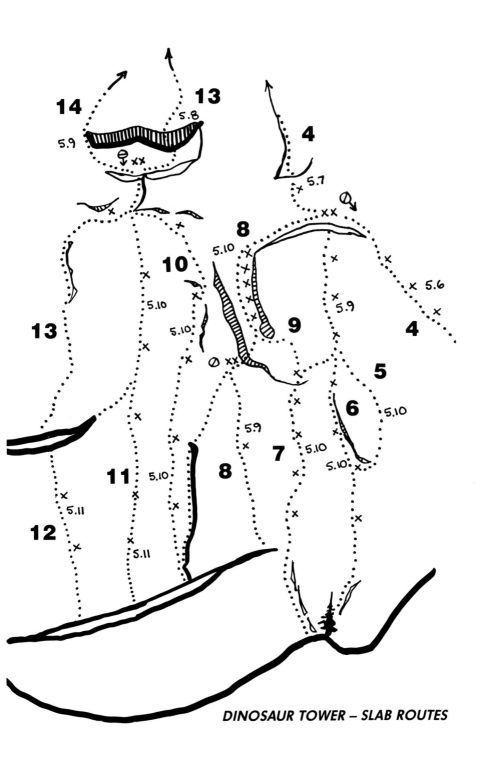

DINOSAUR TOWER – SLAB ROUTES

SUNSET SLAB

Downhill and west from Dinosaur Tower is this small slab which has several moderate friction routes. Descend by tunneling down the backside, or rappelling from ledge. Not shown. Routes are easily distinguishable.

1. **CONTINUOUS BULLSHIT**   *5.6 or 5.9 (R)*
   On right margin of slab, climb to bolt. Go right to have fun, left to get scared. Marginal fixed protection. FA: Steve Ansell, Rich Doorish, 1971.

2. **GREEN VELVET**   ★ **5.8 (R)**
   From right of large tree, climb up flakes to groove up slab. Minimal protection; take small nuts. Somewhat runout at crux. FA: Al Givler.

3. **NATIONAL VELVET**   ★★ **5.6**
   Friction past bolt line in center of slab. Second pitch climbs up gully. Fixed protection. FA: Don Harder.

4. **BOOBY VINTON**   ★ **5.5**
   Friction past bolt line left of National Velvet. Belay at tree ledge. FA: unknown.

5. **SUNSET**   **5.4**
   Groove left of tree leads to tree ledge. Second pitch goes through crack with tree on left. Protection to 3". FA: Fred Beckey, Steve Johnson.

6. **SUNRISE**   **5.7**
   Climb over bulge to bolts on slab (unprotected crux). Belay is on left ledge. Protection to 2". FA: Dan Davis, Dick Springgate.

AUSTRIAN SLAB

Austrian Slab is located directly downhill from Dinosaur Tower. It can be easily reached by traversing southeasterly from Sunset Slab, or by crossing the ridge and descending from Sickle Slab. Descents are made by walking off either side (scrambling), or by rappelling.

1. **SLENDER THREAD**   ★★★ **5.9 (R)**
   Fine friction route on left side of slab, above tree. Has 15-foot bouldering start with bad fall potential. Protection should include an alert spotter. Bolts. FA: Rich Doorish.

2. **FAKIN' IT**   ★★★ **5.10a**
   Friction pitch right of Slender Thread. Shares first bolt with Cajun Queen. Mildly runout. Bolts. FA: Mark Weigelt, Mead Hargis, 1971.

3. **CAJUN QUEEN**   ★★ **5.10a (R)**
   Friction pitch right of shared bolt. Somewhat runout on easy ground. Bolts. FA: Pat Timson, Mead Hargis, 1971.

4. **AUSTRIAN SLAB**   ★ **5.8 (R)**
   Climb grooves and solution pockets up center of slab. Somewhat runout at beginning. Fixed protection; bring a few nuts. FA: Fred Beckey, Eric Bjørnstad, Don Gordon.

5. **LICHEN DELIGHT**   **5.9 (R)**
   Friction pitch right of the standard route. Minimal fixed protection. FA: Bob McGowan.

6. **SLAKIN**   ★ **5.8 (R)**
   Climb solution holes on right side of slab to good friction finish. 25 feet to first bolt. Bolts. FA: Don Brooks, Rick LeDuc, 1975.

SICKLE SLAB

Sickle Slab is the integral formation right of Austrian Slab, lying on the ridge crest between Martian Slab and Orchard Rock. Descents are made by rappelling down Windward Direct, or by rappelling or downclimbing off the back.

1. **THE TREE** (– ★★) **5.4**
   Rotten gully left of Windward Direct. FA: Who cares?

2. **WINDWARD DIRECT** ★★ **5.8**
   Climb steep grooves past bolts on left side of slab. Fixed protection. FA: Dan Davis, Curtis Stout.

3. **WINDWARD 5.6**
   Start as for Direct, then traverse rightward across face and back across ridge. Two pitches. Direct start is 5.8. Fixed protection. FA: Eric Bjørnstad, Pat Callis.

4. **WINDCAVE 5.8**
   Traverse right along crack/ramp into cave, then up slab and along crest. Fixed protection, nuts and slings. FA: Fred Beckey, Eric Bjørnstad.

5. **TESTICLE FORTITUDE** ★ **5.9 (R)**
   Face pitch starting below cave and continuing directly to ridge crest. Fixed protection. FA: Brent Hoffman, Gary Jones.

6. **POISONED KOOL-AID 5.9 (X)**
   Friction left of Testicle Fortitude with very poor protection, including taped skyhooks. FA: Mike Jakubal (rope-solo), 1983.

7. **ROTGUT CRACK** (– ★★) **5.7 (not shown)**
   Deep, rotten crack downhill from cave. FA: who cares?

8. **BURNING SPEAR 5.6 (not shown)**
   On back of slab, bouldering start gains a short crack that leads to the ridge crest. Protection to 4". FA: unknown.

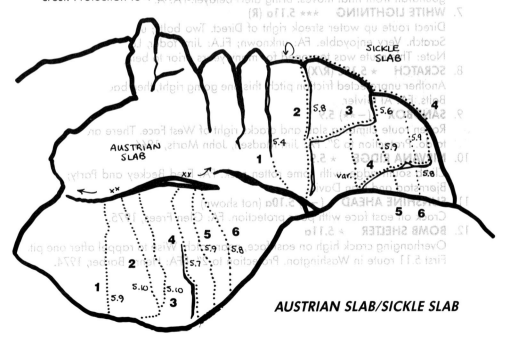

AUSTRIAN SLAB/SICKLE SLAB

GRAND CENTRAL TOWER

Grand Central Tower is the large slab/pinnacle located adjacent to the orchard at the west entrance, just downhill from Sunset Slab. The front face is some 300 feet high and slabby, while the backside is 80 to 120 feet high and overhanging. Descents are by rappel from the Vertigo notch (80 feet) or Empire State ledge (100 feet).

1. **MADSEN'S BUTTRESS**   **(−★★) 5.10+ A0 (X)**
   Leftmost buttress with a few bolts. Actively decomposing rock. This route is not in the same condition as on early ascents. FA: Jim Madsen.

2. **LIGHTNING CRACK**   **★★★ 5.8**
   Two pitch route starting in corner right of Madsen's Buttress. Continue up bolted slab and the Lightning Crack, to ledge and rappel anchors. A Peshastin classic. Protection to 2″. FA: Fred Beckey, Dick McGowan, 1960; FFA: Beckey, 1962.

3. **MIGRANT WORKER   5.10a (X)**
   Right of Lightning Crack is this poorly protected climb that passes overhangs. Protection useless. Taped skyhooks. FA: Mike Jakubal (rope-solo), 1983.

4. **SHADY LANE   5.9**
   Climb crack/groove left of West Face bolts to cave. Continue on rotten rock right and up. Protection to 3″. FA: Clint Cummins, Dave Chin, 1975.

5. **WEST FACE   ★ 5.8**
   The most over-bolted pitch at Peshastin (with the possible exception of Primate). Climb easy slab to bolt belay in dish. Continue up rotten rock through a chimney and finish via one of two variations, both 5.6. Better to rappel from ledge. Protection to 3″. FA: Dave Collins, T. Miller; FFA: Fred Beckey.

6. **WEST FACE DIRECT   ★ 5.10c (R/X)**
   Friction pitch right of bolt line. Two bolts in 80 feet of climbing. Potential for goundfall from final moves. Bring alert belayer. FA: Al Givler, Ron Burgner.

7. **WHITE LIGHTNING   ★★★ 5.11a (R)**
   Direct route up water streak right of Direct. Two bolts; use first bolt of Direct or Scratch. Very enjoyable. FA: unknown; FLA: Jim Yoder, Lee Cunningham, 1986. Note: This route was toproped for many years prior to being bolted and led.

8. **SCRATCH   ★ 5.10c (R/X)**
   Another unprotected friction pitch, this one going right, then back along a groove. Bolts. FA: Al Givler.

9. **SANDBOX   (−★★) 5.9**
   Rotten route climbing slab and cracks right of West Face. There are better things to do. Protection to 3″. FA: Jim Madsen, John Marts, 1966.

10. **NIRVANA RIDGE   ★ 5.9**
    Climb south ridge, with some rotten rock. FA: Fred Beckey and Party; FFA: Eric Bjørnstad and Dan Davis.

11. **SUNSHINE AHEAD   (−★) 5.10a** (not shown)
    Crack on east face with poor protection. FA: Glen Frees, 1975.

12. **BOMB SHELTER   ★ 5.11a**
    Overhanging crack high on east face, near notch. Wise to rappel after one pitch. First 5.11 route in Washington. Protection to 2″. FFA: Henry Barber, 1974.

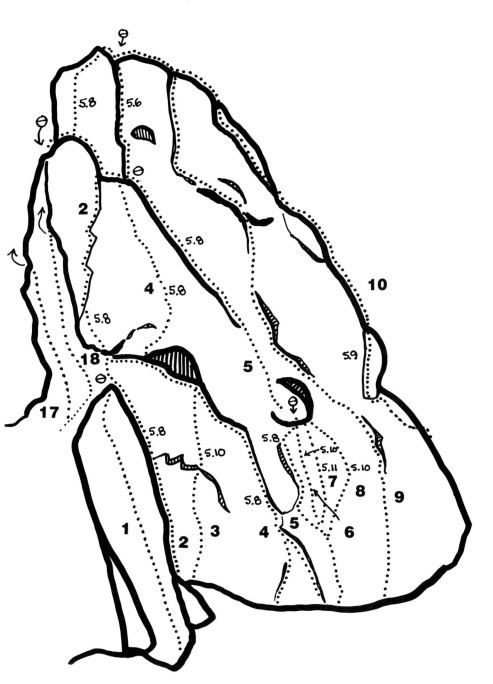

GRAND CENTRAL TOWER – WEST FACE

13. **TIME PASSAGES   5.10d (R/X)**
Sandy pitch between Vertigo and Bomb Shelter. Flaring Friend placements, fixed pins (X-rated if fixed protection fails). FA: Jim Yoder, Lee Cunningham, 1981.
14. **VERTIGO   ★ 5.8**
Steep jam crack leads to flaring chimney to notch. May be poor rappel anchors. Protection to 3". FFA: Fred Beckey, Charles Bell.
15. **CORKSCREW   ★ 5.9**
Overhanging buckets just right of Vertigo, followed by rightward traverse to Empire State. The final pitch to the summit block is neither popular nor well protected. Protection to 2". FA: J. Henry and party, 1949; FFA: Fred Beckey, Joe Hieb.
16. **EMPIRE STATE   5.7**
Traverse across cave to wide crack and chimney. Protection to 3". FA: Fred Beckey, Dick Springgate, Norm Weber.
17. **FAT MAN'S CHIMNEY (aka JOCK TRAP)   5.9**
First obvious chimney downhill from Vertigo. Protection to 2". FA: Fred Stanley, Bruce Schuler, 1965.
18. **ALLEY OOP CHIMNEY   5.9**
Second chimney. Some climbers have been unable to find this route. Protection to 2". FA: Fred Beckey, Eric Bjørnstad.

CHURCH TOWER (not shown)

Church Tower is an isolated slab about 100 yards west of Grand Central Tower. Descend by walking off the back. There are two routes.
1. **CHIMNEY SWEEP   (−★) 5.7**
Rotten, lefthand route on Church Tower. Bolts. FA: Dave Beckstead and Party.
2. **STEEPLE   5.7**
Groove on right side. Bolts. FA: Dan Davis, Dick Springgate.

VULTURE SLAB (not shown)

This is the rotten slab between Grand Central Tower and Church Tower.
1. **THE VULTURE   (−★★) 5.8**
Climbs white groove in center of slab. Bolts. FA: Fred Beckey, Charles Bell.
2. **CONDOR   (−★★) 5.8**
More decomposing friction. Left of Vulture. FA: Ed Vervoort.
3. **BUZZARD   (−★★) 5.4**
And more. Farther left. FA: Ed Vervoort.

DONALD DUCK (not shown)

Small boulder near Vulture Slab. A few routes can be done on it. Has been climbed "no hands." First no hands ascent: Eric Bjørnstad, Milan Fiala, 1963.

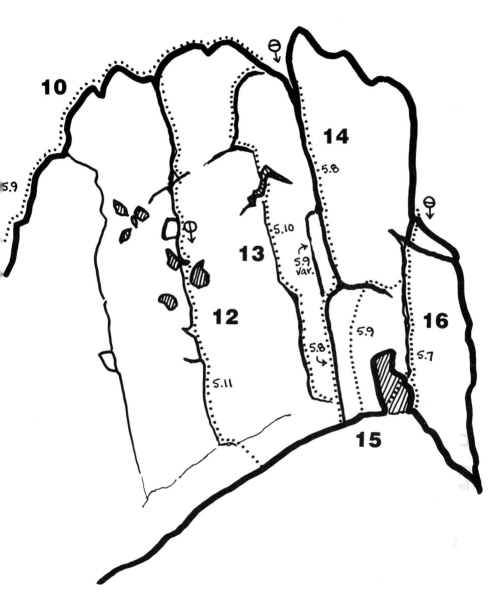

GRAND CENTRAL TOWER – NOTCH AREA

SANDY SLAB

Located 2 miles east of Leavenworth on U.S. 2 is this small, decomposing sandstone slab, on the right, across from a wide parking area. Few climbers visit this conspicuous slab, but it is there if you really miss climbing at Peshastin. All routes are bolted.

1. **GET YOUR WINGS   5.8**
   On the far left. Descent by walking left or rappelling. FA: Bob McGowan 1978.
2. **NEVER ON SUNDAY   5.7**
   Just right of Get Your Wings, climb a "flaky depression" to belay tree. FA: Mark Weigelt 1969.
3. **A-1   5.6**
   Two pitches (80', 150') right of Never on Sunday. Look for aluminum bolt hangers on first pitch. FA: Mark Weigelt 1969.
4. **I SHOT MY BABY   5.8**
   Thirty feet right of A-1, climb to a bolt 25 feet up, then head left to an obvious pine (165'). FA: Don Brooks, Steve Van Mowrick 1978.
5. **FASCIST RULE   5.8 (R)**
   Go right from previously mentioned bolt. Poorly protected. FA: Bob McGowan 1978.
6. **SUNCUPS   ★ 5.8+**
   A well-named line on the far right side, the best pitch on the slab. FA: Bob McGowan 1978.

SHIT SLAB (not shown)

Near Peshastin, on the way to Derby Canyon, is this aptly named slab. Where paved road takes a right-angle turn left, park on a dirt road and walk up railroad tracks to slab. Two 5.7 routes grace this decomposing formation. Fixed protection; take runners. If you can't find this slab, you are probably better off.

1. **LILIES OF THE FIELD   5.7 (−★★)**
   Left of two obvious corners, climb to iron rods. Two pitches to top. FA: Bob Loomis, Gene Heineman 1980.
2. **CATCHING THE SUN   5.7 (−★★)**
   Between the two corners, climb this line to meet Lilies at the top. FA: Bob Loomis, Gene Heineman 1980.

CHUMSTICK SNAG (not shown)

About four miles north of Leavenworth on the Plain road, turn left into Stromberg Canyon on a marked road. Hike through meadows about ½ mile to reach the pinnacle. Two routes reach the top.

1. **STANDARD ROUTE   5.7**
   Start on the southwest corner of the pinnacle, and climb down to potholes leading to the summit. Protection to ¾". FA: Pete Schoening, Tom Miller 1950.
2. **SOUTHWEST FACE   5.8 A1 or 2**
   Mixed free and aid beginning from the upper saddle. FA: Fred Beckey, Steve Marts 1963.

SANDY SLAB

Jim Yoder and Bob Vaughn on Dan's Dreadful Direct, Castle Rock

TUMWATER CANYON

Tumwater Canyon, the deep gorge northwest of Leavenworth, offers some of the finest climbing in Washington, as well as some entertaining kayaking on the Wenatchee River. The canyon, contrary to popular belief, runs mostly north-south, and is protected by a rainshadow from the nearby Stuart Range, making it a dryer alternative to Index on rainy spring days.

Castle Rock is the most obvious of the Tumwater crags, as it is situated directly above the highway about three miles northwest of Leavenworth. In addition to climbers, tourists with binoculars regularly congregate along the guard rails of U.S. 2 to gawk, point and wave. Above Castle looms Midnight Rock and its neighbor, Noontime Rock, and on the ridge above the less-conspicuous and infrequently visited Punk Rock.

Up canyon lie Rattlesnake Rock and Piton Tower, less-visible crags with a steep approach but interesting climbing. Farther up canyon are the big walls of Waterfall Column and Jupiter Rock, with few routes for the acres of available rock. The approach is by walking down one mile from the Tumwater bridge, or by raft or canoe, a risky alternative considering the Grade 6 rapids below.

Also across the river are several crags which have seen little activity. With better access, much could be done. Near town, Tumwater Tower stands out across the river; it is reached by a one mile hike from the bridge one mile down river from Castle Rock.

ROADSIDE ROCK

A large "boulder" perched beside the road just inside the canyon from Leavenworth, with obvious lightning-bolt crack.

  1. **EVERY INCH IS HARD (aka EVERY INCH IS SILLY)   5.12 (TR)**
      The difficult, thin crack. FA: Dick Cilley, 1983.

ROADSIDE ROCK

TUMWATER TOWER (not shown)

Tumwater Tower is a small pinnacle located about 1½ miles from Leavenworth, across the river from U.S. 2. It can be reached by crossing the footbridge two miles from town and hiking down beside the river, then up the canyon wall. Descend by rappel. The tower may be difficult to spot from below. Reconnoiter the approach before starting to save time and trouble.

1. **NORMAL ROUTE** ⋆ **5.5**
   Climb a dihedral on the inside face. Protection to 2". FA: Fred Beckey and party.
2. **UPPER NOTCH ROUTE** **5.6**
   Start at the notch and climb onto the north face. Protection to 2". FA: Pete Schoening, Tom Miller.
3. **HIGHWAY ROUTE** ⋆ **5.8**
   An obvious route on the highway face. Protection to 2". FA: Fred Beckey, Eric Bjørnstad, 1962; FFA: Rick LeDuc, 1973.
4. **HIGHWAY DIRECT** **5.10b**
   Cracks on the southeast face. Protection unknown. FA: Jim Yoder, Lee Cunningham, George Rohrbach.
5. **SOUTHEAST FACE** **5.10b**
   Two pitch route. FA: Jim Yoder, Paul Christensen.

There are several routes on the lower face. Only the first ascent teams can tell which is which. Since they are each as difficult as the others, it doesn't matter. Look for bolts to find these routes.

6. **PIN HEAD** **5.10b**
   FA: Paul Christensen, Jim Yoder.
7. **CONE HEAD** **5.10b**
   FA: Lee Cunningham, George Rohrback, Jim Yoder.
8. **MONGO** **5.10b**
   Two pitches. FA: Paul Christensen, Jim Yoder.
9. **GYM** **5.10**
   FA: George Rohrbach, Lee Cunningham.

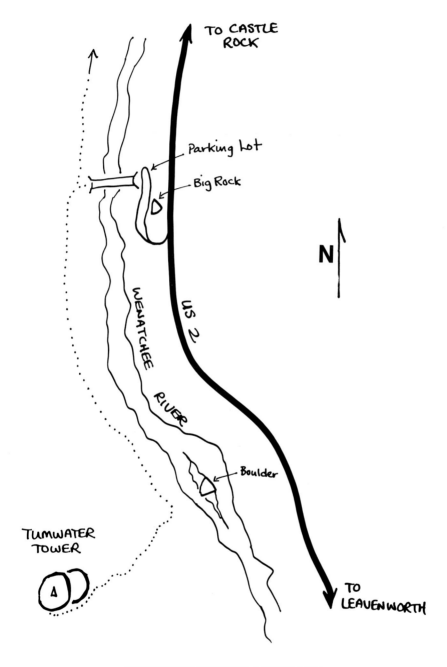

TUMWATER TOWER APPROACH

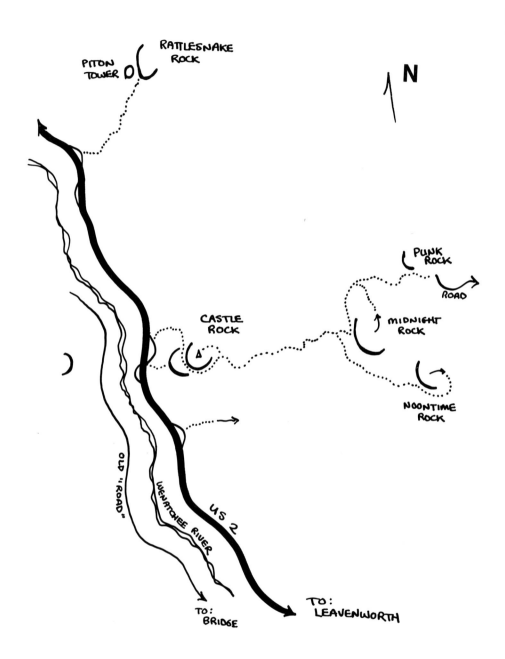

CASTLE ROCK AREA

CASTLE ROCK

CASTLE ROCK

Castle Rock is the obvious roadside crag located about three miles outside of Leavenworth on U.S. 2. It is indisputably the most popular crag in the Leavenworth area. It is split in half by Logger's Ledge, a broad shelf which provides access and descent for and from most of the routes on the crag. Descents are made by walking down and right (southeast) from the summit.

UPPER CASTLE ROCK

Upper Castle Rock is the portion of the crag rising above Logger's Ledge, a wide shelf traversing the rock at mid-height. The lower left side of Upper Castle is blocky and mostly overhanging, while the right side is vertical or less, and more fractured. Jello Tower is the squat 100-foot-high tower perched in the middle of Logger's Ledge. Be careful not to kick rocks off of Logger's Ledge, as there are usually climbers below.

Descents are made down the trail leading from the summit to the right (south). Rappel anchors are in place atop Jello Tower.

1. **NORTH RIDGE   5.5** (not shown)

   Rarely climbed route on left skyline. Probably mossy and blocky. Protection unknown. FA: Paul Myhre, Roger Osborn, 1967.

2. **NORTHWIND   5.10d (PG-13)**

   Takes the line of the original aid route through blocky rock and a huge roof. From the ramp on the left side of the cliff, traverse left onto the blocky wall and up face and corners. The route climbs through the previously A4 roof with the crux above. Protection is difficult above the roof. Protection to 3". FA: Jim Stuart, B. Sprenger; FFA: Lee Cunningham, Jim Yoder, 1984.

3. **RAINSHADOW   5.12a**

   Start up the Northwind ramp, then climb a vertical, blocky wall to an obvious overhanging flake leading to a ledge with a tree. Continue up the overhanging wall above to easier climbing. The route continues up face and around roofs higher up. Protection to 2". FA: Fred Beckey, Eric Bjørnstad, Jim Stuart; FFA: Greg Child, Matt Kerns, Jim Yoder, 1985.

4. **DAS MUSAK   5.11d**

   Blocky face climb through roofs which reaches the small tree of Rainshadow. Starts atop boulder. Protection to 2"; fixed pins. FA: Perry Beckham, 1985.

5. **RAINBOW CONNECTION   ★ 5.11b**

   Blocky face climb right of Das Musak, passing roofs higher up. Starts atop boulder. Protection to 1". FA: Dan Lepeska, Mike Adams, 1980; FFA: Jim Yoder.

6. **BY THE SEA   5.10c**

   Short offering between Rainbow Connection and Saints. Traverse left from Saints to connect with Saints higher up. Protection to 1". FA: Pat Littlejohn, 1978.

7. **SAINTS   ★★★ 5.8+**

   Start up the obvious short corner (crux), continuing left through blocks to the tree ledge. Continue right and up a blocky face and dihedrals, straying right of the arete onto face climbing and the top. Protection to 2". FA: Fred Beckey and party, 1957; FFA: Steve Marts, Pat Callis, 1963.

8. **SHORT 'N SASSY   5.9+**

   Link Saints corner and Angel belay ledge via short crack. Protection to 1". FA: Jim Yoder, 1981.

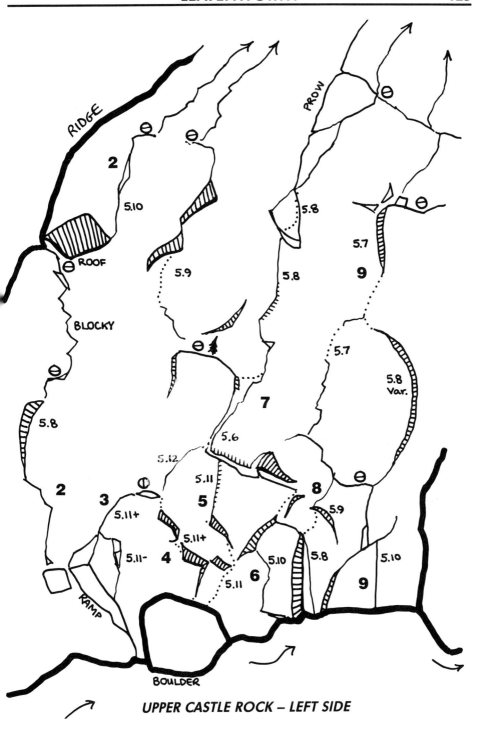

UPPER CASTLE ROCK – LEFT SIDE

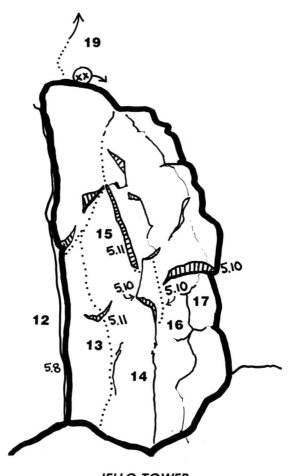

JELLO TOWER

9. **ANGEL** ★★★ **5.10b**
   Starts with an obvious thin crack (crux) to a ledge, then left and up a blocky face
   to a short dihedral. Continue rightward to top. Protection to 1". This route has
   traditionally been rated 5.7, as the crux is a boulder problem. FA: Pete Schoening,
   Jim Henry; FFA: Fred Beckey, Don Gordon.

10. **SIMPERING WHIMPS**   **5.11a** (not shown)
    Climb Angel crack, then continue up and right, crossing **Damnation** and joining
    M.F. Direct at the roof. Contrived and obscure route. Protection to 1". FA: Dan
    Lepeska, Scott Northey, 1985.

11. **DAN'S DREADFUL DIRECT**   **5.11d (R)**
    A former aid route which is now a dangerous and somewhat contrived face climb
    between **Angel** and **Damnation**. Take multiple sets of RPs. FA: Dan Davis, Pat
    Callis, 1963; FFA: Dan Lepeska, John Stoddard, 1985 (credit where credit is due:
    Jim Yoder almost led it free the day before Lepeska's free lead).

JELLO TOWER

The following eight routes (12 through 19) are located on Jello Tower. Midway and Midway Direct begin directly atop the pillar. Rappel anchors are in place for easy descents to Logger's Ledge.

12. **DAMNATION** ★ **5.8**
   Corner crack right of Angel featuring liebacking, stemming and jamming. FA: John Rupley, 1957; FFA: TM Herbert, Ed Cooper, 1960.

13. **NO SUCH THING AS A FREE LUNGE** ★ **5.11d (R)**
   A dangerous lead between Damnation and M.F. on Jello Tower, taking a blank, bulging face to the higher roof. "The longest possible fall is 20 feet, if protection holds . . . ." Marginal protection including Friends and RPs. FA: Dick Cilley (TR); FLA: Dan Lepeska, 1983.

14. **M.F. OVERHANG** ★★★ **5.10c**
   An excellent climb up a thin crack through an overhang. Starts on the lefthand prow of Jello Tower. Protection to 1". FA: Ed Cooper, Gordon Thompson; FFA: Al Givler.

15. **M.F. DIRECT** ★★★ **5.11b (PG-13)**
   After the crux of M.F., move left into a leaning dihedral to a roof. Protection to 1", with small RPs. FA: Peter Croft, 1983.

16. **SLIM PICKINS** ★ **5.10c**
   Short variation going right to "avoid" roof of M.F. Protection to ½". FA: Jim Yoder, Lee Cunningham, 1984.

17. **THE NOSE** ★★★ **5.10d**
   Excellent climb up cracks to the roof on "front" face of Jello Tower. Variation escapes right below roof (5.10c) onto true "Nose." Protection to 1". FA: Fred Beckey, Don Gordon, Ed Cooper, 1959; FFA: Mead Hargis.

18. **SOUTH FACE** ★ **5.8**
   Obvious crack on south (right) face of Jello Tower. A variation climbs face to wide crack right from bolt (rating unknown). Protection to 2". FA: Joe Hieb et al.; FFA: Fred Beckey, D. Collins, 1962.

19. **MIDWAY** ★★ **5.5**
   A classic Castle Rock outing, even if there are better routes to be found. Climb chimney on right side of Jello Tower, step across, then right and up wide crack to top. Protection to 2". FA: Fred Beckey, Wes Grande, Jack Schwabland, 1948.

20. **MIDWAY DIRECT** ★ **5.6 (R)**
   An exposed face climb left of Midway. Head straight up the dihedral after doing the step across, then move left onto exposed face. From ledge, several variations to the top are possible. Protection to 2". FA: TM Herbert, Eric Bjørnstad, R. Neufer, 1960.

21. **WINTER SOLSTICE** ★ **5.6**
   Climb ramp right of Jello Tower to ledge beneath overhangs, then traverse left to almost meet Midway. Exposed, continuous face climbing parallels Midway on the right to the top. Protection to 2". FA: Eric Bjørnstad, B. Hooper.

22. **BODY & SOUL** **5.11b**
   Silly two-move climb just left of Devil's Fright, through roof. Protection unknown. FA: Dick Cilley, Jim Yoder, 1983.

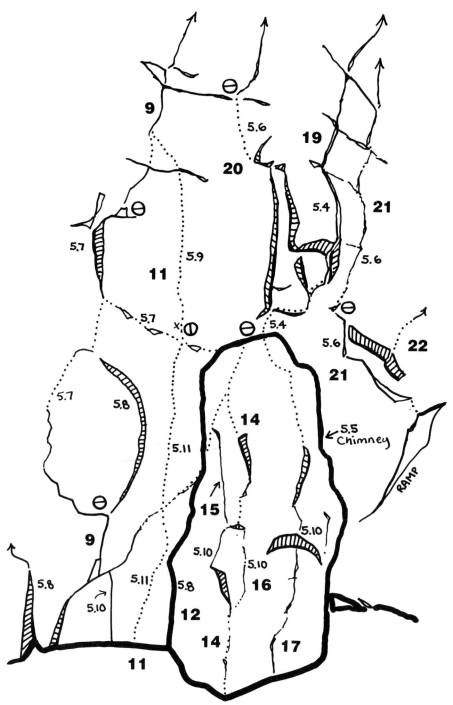

UPPER CASTLE ROCK – JELLO TOWER AREA

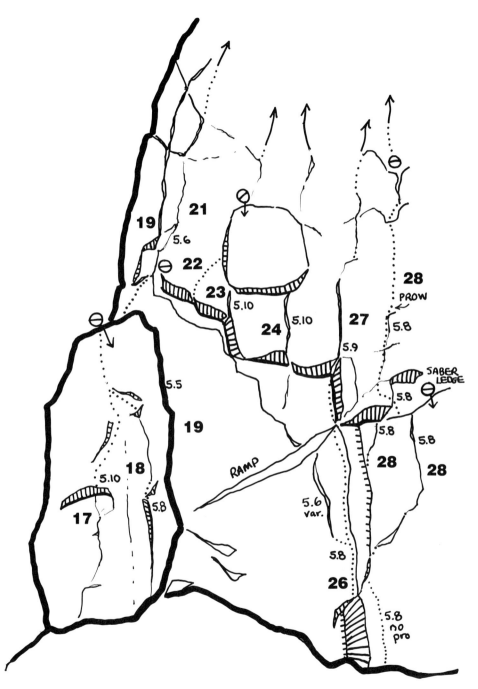

UPPER CASTLE ROCK – CANARY AREA

23. **DEVIL'S FRIGHT** ★ **5.10b**
Blocky roof at top of ramp right of Jello Tower. Continue up steep rock to the top. Protection to 1½". FA: Ed Cooper, TM Herbert; FFA: Jim Madsen, Ron Burgner, 1966.

24. **DEVIL'S DELIGHT** ★ **5.10c**
White, blocky wall to roof right of Devil's Fright. Protection to 1". FA: Fred Beckey, Pete Schoening, Wes Grande. FFA: Jim Madsen, Tom Hargis, 1966.

25. **THE DEVIL MADE ME DO IT** **5.10c** (not shown)
Traverse from Devil's Fright to Delight under roof. Protection to 1". FA: Dan Lepeska, Mike Jakubal, 1983.

26. **OLD GREY MARE** ★★★ **5.8**
An excellent pitch leading up the arete below Crack of Doom. Protection to 1". FA: Dan Davis.

27. **CRACK OF DOOM** ★★★ **5.9+**
The crack through the blocky roof at the right edge of the ramp leads to exposed face climbing. Protection to 2½". FA: Dan Davis; FFA: Jim Madsen.

28. **CANARY** ★★★ **5.8 (PG-13/R)**
Starts at Old Grey Mare and climbs to Saber Ledge via two variations: 1) Direct: Climb straight up dihedral and traverse right under roof; 2) Traverse right from corner and climb face cracks. Second pitch traverses left across overhang to exposed face (scary!). Protection to 2". FA: Fred Beckey, Dave Collins, Don Gordon, 1957; FFA: H. Mather, J. Rupley.

29. **HANGDOG** **5.11a/b (R)**
Poorly protected face right of the start of Canary leads to a small roof. Continue up thin, pocketed cracks to Saber Ledge. Protection to 2". FA: Jim Yoder, 1982.

30. **CAT BURGLAR** ★ **5.6**
A bouldering move gains an obvious ramp. Traverse right then back left up shallow cracks to reach Saber Ledge. Continue up face and cracks on right. Protection to 2". FA: Fred Beckey, Don Gordon, John Rupley, 1957.

31. **DIRETISSIMA** ★ **5.7**
Discontinuous, shallow face cracks left of Saber. Continues above Saber Ledge. Protection to 1". FA: Eric Bjørnstad, Ed Cooper, 1960.

32. **SABER** ★★ **5.4**
Another classic "easy" route. At right end of Logger's Ledge, climb left over buttress into dihedral, then cracks to ledge. Continue straight up chimney to easy face and cracks to top. Protection to 2". FA: Pete Schoening, Dick Widrig, 1949.

33. **ORANGE PEEL** **5.9**
Horizontal face crack in left wall of Saber chimney. Joins Canary. Protection to 2". FA: Jim Yoder, 1980.

34. **CENTURY** ★★★ **5.8**
A continuous face climb up blunt arete right of first pitch of Saber. Many old fixed pins. Protection to 2". FA: Ed Cooper, Ron Priebe, Bruce Gibbs, 1959; FFA: Eric Bjørnstad, Ed Cooper, 1960.

35. **ROOFER** **5.9 (R)**
Right of Century, climb past bolt on slab through two somewhat rotten roofs. Protection to 2". FA: Rick Graham, Brian Scott, 1980.

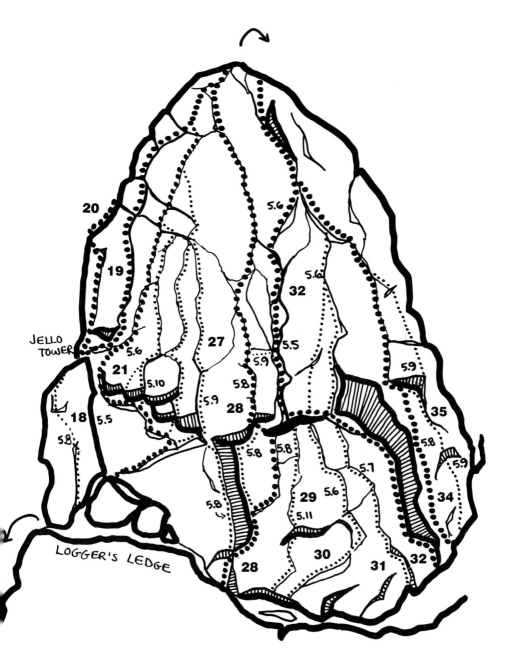

UPPER CASTLE ROCK – RIGHT SIDE

LOWER CASTLE ROCK

Lower Castle is the blocky, roof-infested cliff below Logger's Ledge. A short trail from the right side of the parking lot leads to the Fault chimney. Descents are usually made by walking down from Logger's Ledge. Beware of rockfall from above.

1. **CLEM'S LAYBACK   5.8**
   A short, mossy flake/dihedral on the far left side. Protection to 2". FA: Jim Yoder, Peter Austin, 1979.

2. **APESVILLE   5.12a**
   Mossy, thin crack through initial overhangs on left side. Second pitch goes through higher overhang on left side. Protection to 1". FA: Jim Yoder, Peter Austin, 1980; Second Pitch: Jim Yoder, Bob Vaughan, 1982-1986.

3. **MONKEY LIP   ★ 5.11d**
   Roofs right of Apesville. Cleaner, with fixed pins. Starts just left of Brass Balls, and climbs through two roofs. Think like a monkey to succeed on the first crux. Protection to 1". FA: Peter Croft, Jim Yoder, 1981.

4. **BRASS BALLS   ★★★ 5.10b**
   Double roofs lead to blocky dihedral. A classic. Protection to 2". FA: Jim Yoder, Paul Christiansen, 1980.

5. **SHRIEK OF THE MUTILATED   ★ 5.12a**
   Obvious thin crack splitting roofs right of Brass Balls. Protection to 2". FA: Peter Croft, Jim Yoder, 1981.

6. **GLORY DAYS   5.11c**
   Roof pitch squeezed in between Shriek and Catapult. Protection to 2". FA: Jim Yoder, Pat McNerthney, 1984.

7. **CATAPULT   ★★ 5.8**
   Exposed roof and dihedral up the middle of the cliff, directly above the Fault chimney. Protection to 2". FA: Jim Stuart, B.D. Nelson.

8. **MR. CLEAN   ★ 5.10c** (not shown)
   Short, well-scrubbed face cracks and ledges left of the Fault chimney. Protection to 1". FA: Jim Yoder, Phil Rainwater, 1980.

9. **SMUT   ★ 5.10a (PG-13)** (not shown)
   Steep, thin face climb up center of lower face, left of the Fault chimney. Small wired nuts. Friable flakes. FA: Dan Lepeska, John Tarver, 1980.

10. **ULTRA-BRITE   5.10b (R/X)** (not shown)
    Face pitch up right side of face, just left of the Fault chimney. Use bolt on Smut, then long runout right to a fixed pin (if it is there). Ground fall possible before pin. Friable rock. FA: Jim Yoder, 1982 (TR); FLA: Yoder, 1983.

11. **THE FAULT   5.6**
    The obvious central chimney leads to right-wandering ramps and ledges which skirt the overhangs on the right. The route is somewhat dirty. Hint: Stay high on ramps to short dihedral rather than continuing right on main ledge system. At top, either traverse off or climb a 5.6 dihedral directly to Logger's Ledge. Protection to 3". FA: Eric Bjørnstad, Ed Cooper, 1960.

12. **THE VERTEBRAE   5.10b**
    Thin crack through blocky roof straight above Stoners' Ledge (marked on photo). Protection to 1". FA: Jim Yoder, Rick Hoven, Paul Christiansen, 1979.

Midway

Logger's Ledge

Stoner's Ledge

LOWER CASTLE ROCK – LEFT SIDE

13. **THE BONE (aka PENSTEMON)** ★★★ **5.9**
Goes right from Catapult where that route goes left. Go right out roof (5.8) and up to cracks, then through spectacular roof (The Spike). Continue up a blocky wall to Logger's Ledge. Protection to 3". FA: Eric Bjørnstad, Dave Hiser; FFA: Jim Yoder, Paul Christiansen, 1979.

14. **GORE ROOF**　**5.10b**
Roof crack with small tree right of The Bone. Protection to 2". FA: Jim Yoder, Gordon Briody, 1979.

15. **J.J. OVERHANG**　**5.10d**
Roof crack farther right. Approach from the right. Protection to 2". FA: Jim Donini, Jim Yoder, 1979.

16. **SQUEAK OF THE HUMILIATED (aka SPECTATOR OVERHANG)**　**5.12b**
Original line of Spectator Overhang, free climbing the long roof crack above The Fault, right of J.J. Very obvious. Protection to 2". FA: Eric Bjørnstad, Guido Magnone, Les McDonald, Jean Coure, 1962; FFA: Todd Skinner, 1983.

17. **GORILLA DESPERADO**　★ **5.11a/b (R)**
Face variation to Spectator Overhang which utilizes a flake to avoid the hard climbing of the crack itself. Protection to 2". Note: Some parties pre-protect by aiding the roof crack. FFA: Peter Croft, Jim Yoder, 1983.

18. **IDIOT'S DELIGHT**　**5.9**
Face climb out overhangs from left end of ledge near end of The Fault. Fairly obvious when you get there. Protection to 2". FA: John Rupley, Joe Hieb, 1957; FFA: Eric Bjørnstad, Ed Cooper, 1960.

19. **BIRD'S NEST OVERHANG**　**5.8**
Obvious thin roof crack in corner at far right end of The Fault ledges. Protection to 2". FA: Fred Beckey, Tom Hornbein, 1957; FFA: Jim McCarthy, Jim Langdon, 1968.

20. **CLEAN LOVE**　**5.10b**
Face cracks just right of The Fault chimney. Protection to 2". FA: Doug and Karen Klewin, 1980.

21. **AIDS VICTIM**　★ **5.10c**
A bolted pitch just right of Clean Love. Protection to 1½". FA: Jim Yoder 1988.

22. **AMY CARTER**　**5.9** (not shown)
Scruffy crack route right of AIDS Victim. Not popular. Protection to 2". FA: Jim Yoder, 1980.

23. **FLYING FROG**　**5.9** (not shown)
Likewise, only farther right. Protection to 2". FA: Jim Yoder, Paul Christiansen, 1980.

24. **DR. EGO BONER**　**5.10b** (not shown)
On the far right side, this is another new bolted pitch. Protection to 2". FA: Jim Yoder 1988.

LOWER CASTLE ROCK – RIGHT SIDE

Mr. Clean, Lower Castle Rock

MIDNIGHT ROCK

Midnight Rock is the large formation perched atop the ridge above Castle Rock in the Tumwater Canyon. This massive block of granite has some of the finest crack routes in Washington, but is sparsely visited due to the length and/or complexity of the approach.

A trail leads right from the top of Castle Rock and climbs the steep, sandy canyon wall to the cliff, a trip that takes about 45 minutes. It is easy to get lost near the end of the trail. Hint: When bushes appear on the right and a box canyon appears on the left, scramble over a rocky buttress into the brush and you will find the trail.

Alternatively, for those with a junk car or 4x4, there is a poor road that climbs from Leavenworth to the ridge crest near Punk Rock, making for a pleasant 15 minute downhill walk to the cliff. The road is obvious from town.

Descents from the top can be made by walking left (northwest) down a trail. Rappel anchors are installed on many of the major ledges. Dead End Ledge is reached via an exposed Class 4 traverse rightward from the base of Yellow Bird. The lower routes, and Noontime Rock, can be reached on a trail that leads below the main cliff.

1. **CORNER CRACK   5.9**
   Short dihedral crack on block left of Midnight Rock. Protection to 2". FA: unknown.
2. **CURTAINS   ★★★ 5.10a**
   Popular one pitch crack climb on the upper left wall. Protection to 3". FA: Kjell Swedin, Bob McDougall, 1979.
3. **NORTH RAMP   5.10**
   Cracks on left side leading to long ramp near prow. Protection to 3" Rating unknown; may have aid moves. FA: Dave Becksted, Art Amot, 1963; FFA: Manuel Gonzales.
4. **NIGHTINGALE   ★ 5.11+**
   Steep thin cracks starting with a small roof left of Yellow Bird. Rating uncertain. Protection to 1". FA: Fred Beckey, Dave Becksted, 1964; FFA: Pat Timson, Pete Doorish.
5. **YELLOW BIRD   ★★ 5.9**
   Start up a short roof with a flake, traverse right, and up thin crack to V.W. Ledge. Two chimney variations lead off the ledge (left chimney is harder). Protection to 2". FA: Jim Stuart, Dave Becksted, 1963; FFA: Don McPherson, Tom Hargis.
6. **TWILIGHT ZONE   5.11c (PG-13)**
   Bolt-protected face at left end of Dead End Ledge leads through hard-to-protect roof and wide cracks to V.W. Ledge. Protection to 4". FA: Tim Wilson, Lee Cunningham, Jim Yoder, 1984.
7. **SOMETIMES A GREAT NOTION   ★★★ 5.10d**
   Thin crack leading left from above start of Wild Traverse to right edge of V.W. Ledge. Protection to 1". FA: Kjell Swedin, Bob McDougall, 1980.
8. **BLACK WIDOW   ★ 5.10c**
   Wide crack through lefthand roof. Protection to 3". FA: Fred Beckey, Dave Becksted, 1962; FFA: Jim Madsen, Ron Burgner, 1967.
9. **EASTER OVERHANG   ★★★ 5.10a**
   Wide crack directly through middle of roofs. Protection to 4". FA: Jim Stuart, Dave Becksted, 1962; FFA: Jim Madsen, Ron Burgner, 1967.

10. **WILD TRAVERSE**   ★ **5.9**
Longest route at Midnight Rock. Start in a short dihedral at the left end of Dead End Ledge and traverse right across ledges and up dihedrals to the south ramp system on right side of wall (The Apron). Protection to 2″. FA: Fred Beckey, Tom Hornbein, 1957.

11. **IN SEARCH OF THE PERFECT PUMP**   **5.11+**
An athletic, arching roof starting from Dead End Ledge leads to base of Easter Overhang. Protection to 2″. FA: Kjell Swedin, Bob McDougall, 1980.

12. **STEVENS PASS MOTEL**   ★★★ **5.11d**
Obvious long, thin dihedral crack starting with bolt-protected face at right end of Dead End Ledge. Direct finish goes up seam (R). Protection to 1″. FA: Peter Croft, 1984.

13. **TWIN CRACKS**   **5.10c**
Double offwidths at left end of ledge at top of Stevens Pass Motel. Protection to 5″. FA: Fred Beckey, Tom Hornbein, 1957; FFA: Jim Madsen, Kim Schmitz, 1968.

14. **R.O.T.C.**   ★★★★ **5.11c**
Wild, overhanging, thin jamcrack right of Twin Cracks. Protection to 2″. FA: Paul Boving, 1977.

15. **THE DAGOBA SYSTEM**   ★ **5.12a A0 (5.13?)**
Bolted face route right of R.O.T.C., climbing colorful wall to top (has not had a known complete free ascent, i.e. no known redpoint or yo-yo ascent). FA: Martin McBirney, Randell Green 1986.

16. **STING**   ★ **5.10b**
Left of two cracks leading to base of R.O.T.C. from Dead End Ledge system. Protection to 3″. FA: Jim Stuart; FFA: Jim Madsen, Kim Schmitz, 1968.

17. **WASP**   **5.10a**
Wider crack right of Sting. Protection to 4″. FA: Jim Stuart, Bob Phelps, Dave Hiser, 1964; FFA: Jim Madsen, Kim Schmitz, 1968.

18. **THE FLAME**   ★ **5.8**
Traverse rightward from Dead End Ledge to handcrack, which leads to an intimidating traverse into right-hand crack, then up to ledge. Protection to 3″. FA: unknown.

19. **ROLLERCOASTER**   ★ **5.9**
Wavy chimney directly above The Flame. Protection to 2″. FA: Fred Beckey, Don Gordon, Frank Tarver, 1959; FFA: Fred Beckey, Henry Mather, 1963.

20. **PLUMBLINE**   ★ **5.11d**
Steep thin crack system right of Rollercoaster. Protection to 1″. FA: Dan Mc-Merthney, Jim Yoder; FFA: Peter Croft, 1983.

21. **J.A.M. SESSION**   ★ **5.10c**
Traverse right from Plumbline up long flake to steep face, then traverse back left under huge summit block. Protection to 1″. FA: Jay Ossiander, Al Givler, Mead Hargis.

22. **FROG SUICIDE**   **5.10a**
Short roof right of start of The Flame. Protection to 2″. FA: Kjell Swedin, Jeff Baird, 1979.

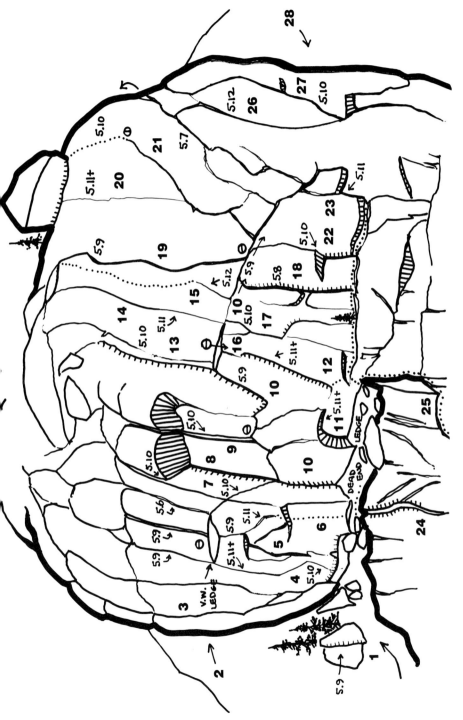

MIDNIGHT ROCK

23. **DIAMOND IN THE ROUGH**   ★ **5.11a**
Wide crack through roof at far end of ledge, right of Frog Suicide. Protection to
4". FA: Kjell Swedin, Bob McDougall, 1980.

24. **MIDNIGHT RAMBLER**   **5.7**
Chimney starting from the ground, reaching the ledge left of the start of Twilight
Zone. Protection to 4". FA: Brent Hoffman, Karl Kaiyala.

25. **MIDNIGHT MADNESS**   **5.8+**
Cracks and face on wall below Dead End Ledge. Largely unknown. Protection
to 3". FA: Brent Hoffman, Karl Kaiyala.

26. **SUPERCRACK**   ★★ **5.12**
Striking, widening crack on right side of Midnight Rock. Fingers, hands and fist,
then offwidth through roof. First 5.12 in Washington. Remains unrepeated. Protection to 5". FA: Pat Timson, 1979.

27. **SOUTH RAMP**   **5.10a**
Steep crack route right of Supercrack, climbing from ground to meet the final
pitches of Wild Traverse at the apron. Protection to 2". FA: Fred Beckey, Dave
Beckstead, 1964; FFA: Jim Madsen.

28. **SPELLBOUND**   ★★ **5.11b**
Thin, overhanging crack on far right side of Midnight Rock. Protection to 1". FA:
Kjell Swedin, Bob McDougall (or Rick LeDuc).

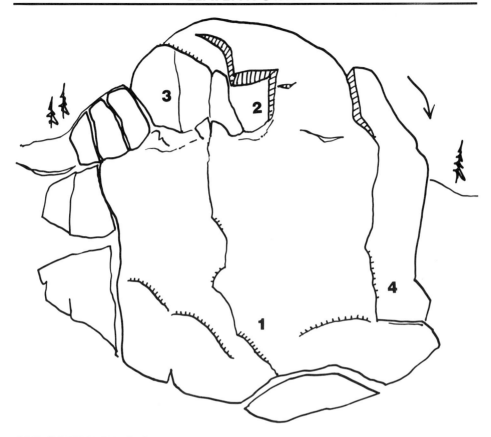

NOONTIME ROCK

Noontime Rock is the large wall right of Midnight Rock on the ridge crest above Castle Rock. It can be reached via the Midnight Rock trail from Castle, or from above as for Midnight Rock. A side trail leads under Midnight Rock, traversing the rocky slope to Noontime.

There are two main routes, Gulliver's Travels and Wall Street, both former aid routes which have had pitches freed over the years. This wall is less fractured than Midnight, so it has fewer climbs.

Descents can be made by walking or scrambling off the right side.

1. **GULLIVER'S TRAVELS**   ★★ **5.12a**
   Long free route starting at lowest point on left side of Noontime Rock. Protection to 3". FA: Eric Bjørnstad, Fred Beckey; FFA: Peter Croft, Dan Lepeska, 1982.

2. **LILLIPUTIAN ROOF**   ★ **5.11a**
   Roof pitch right of upper section of Gulliver's Travels. Protection to 2". FA: Peter Croft, 1982.

3. **SHOOTOUT AT HIGH NOON**   ★ **5.11a**
   Roof on left side accessed by rappelling from tree onto the apron, then climbing flake. Protection to 2". FA: Kjell Swedin, 1981.

4. **WALL STREET**   **5.11 A3**
   First pitch is free; remaining aid pitches continue up right side. Protection to 3". FA: Fred Beckey and Party; FFA: Peter Croft, 1982 (first pitch).

PUNK ROCK (not shown)

Hidden at the ridge crest above Midnight Rock is this small crag. It is best reached by car via the road from Leavenworth, although it can be reached by hiking for one hour from Castle Rock. Punk Rock has several crack climbs, mostly named for AC/DC songs.

1. **TOUCH TOO MUCH** ★ **5.9**
   Roof crack on far left side. Protection to 2". FA: Doug Klewin, Mike Jackson, Dean Geiselman 1979.

2. **HIGHWAY TO HELL** **5.10a**
   Obvious off-width crack on left side. Protection to 4". FA: Doug Klewin, Mike Jackson, Dean Geiselman 1979.

3. **BIG BALLS** **5.11a**
   Corner crack to roof, with crux face above. Protection to 2". FA: Doug Klewin, Dean Geiselman, Dan McNerthney 1979.

4. **DIRTY DEEDS** **A2+**
   Thirty feet of aid leads to a rivet ladder. KBs, LAs, #3½ Friend. FA: Doug Klewin, John Fup 1979.

5. **BEATIN' ROUND THE BUSH** **A2+**
   Aid cracks above a small tree. FA: Doug Klewin (solo) 1979.

6. **SHOT DOWN IN FLAMES** ★ **5.10d**
   Thin crack which widens to off-width. A variation climbs the overhanging hand crack on the left (5.10a). Protection to 4". FA: Mike Jackson, Pat and Dan McNerthney 1979.

7. **ANOTHER AC/DC SONG** **5.11d/5.12a (PG-13)**
   A thin, bolted seam beside Shot Down in Flames. Protection to 2". FA: Jim Yoder, Tobin Kelley.

8. **GIRL'S GOT RYTHYM** ★ **5.8+**
   Right-facing corner to straight-in crack on right side. Protection to 2½". FA: Doug and Karen Klewin 1979.

RATTLESNAKE ROCK (not shown)

Rattlesnake Rock is located on the east wall of Tumwater Canyon, about ¾ mile upriver from Castle Rock. A sandy trail leads from a graded roadside parking area just south of the crag. Descents can be made by walking off the backside. The routes are listed right to left.

1. **SHAKEY PINE** **5.8**
   A dihedral right and uphill from where the trail leads left to Piton Tower. Protection to 2". FA: Eric Bjørnstad, Dave Hiser, 1964.

2. **GANGSTERS** **5.10c/d**
   A somewhat contrived pitch climbing face left of Shakey Pine. Apparently, the trick is to stay off the arete; otherwise it is easier. Bolts? FA: Randy Atkinson, Dean Hart 1987.

3. **VIPER CRACK** **5.8**
   Follow an obvious crack left of Shakey Pine. Variation climbs from a tree to the right and joins the main route after 100 feet. Protection to 2". FA: Don Gordon, Ed Cooper, 1959.

Left of Viper Crack, where the trail splits left towards Piton Tower, are three routes climbing the blocky, overhanging wall. All are bolted Canadian-style (i.e., long runouts).

4. **ZWEIBLES   5.12a (PG-13)**
   The right-most route. Well-spaced bolts, bring TCUs. FA: Tim Wilson 1987.

5. **ROCK 'N' RATTLE   5.11c (PG-13)**
   The middle route. Well-spaced bolts. FA: Dean Hart, Randy Atkinson 1987.

6. **TUBBING AT DER RITTERHOFF   5.11a (R)**
   The left-most route. Possible ground fall on 5.11 moves said to exist. FA: Dean Hart, Randy Atkinson 1987.

The next three routes share a common rappel anchor.

7. **DRILLMEISTER   5.11b/c**
   A bolted face pitch left of Tubbing. Bring TCUs. FA: Matt Kerns, Lee Cunningham 1988.

8. **FOREARM CONFUSION   5.10d (PG-13)**
   Another bolted wall left of Drillmeister. Well-spaced bolts; bring TCUs. FA: Matt Kerns, Jim Yoder 1988.

9. **EARLY ARCHEOLOGIST   5.10a**
   Face climb into a fading crack, with bolts above. Protection to 2". FA: Matt Kerns, Bruce Anderson 1988.

10. **MONTY PYTHON   5.10a/b**
    Discontinuous cracks just right of Piton Tower lead to the top. A long pitch. Protection unknown. FA: Steve Risse, Donna McBain 1988.

11. **NORTHWEST ROUTE   5.0**
    Climb up and left from the notch directly across from Piton Tower. Protection to 3" and slings. FA: Pete Schoening and party.

12. **WEST ROUTE   5.9**
    East (left) of the notch, climb a chimney. Protection to 2". FA: Ed Cooper, Galen McBee.

13. **THE WHIPPET   5.8**
    Diagonal crack direct start to West Route. Protection to 2". FA: Don Brooks, Mark White, 1971.

14. **WILDFLOWER   rating unknown**
    Climb chimney behind boulder east (left and downhill) of notch, then mixed free and aid. Little else known about this route. FA: Paul Myhre, Dave Becksted, 1967.

PITON TOWER   (not shown)

Piton Tower is the detached pinnacle beside Rattlesnake Rock. It has several routes, the easiest being the North (or East) Face route. Of the several aid routes on its other faces, two have gone free. Descend by rappel into notch.

1. **EAST FACE (aka NORTH ROUTE)   5.9**
   From the notch climb cracks and chimney up face and corner to top. Protection to 2". FA: Pete Schoening, Wes Grande, Ralph Widrig, Joe Heib, 1948; FFA: Eric Bjørnstad, Dan Davis, 1961.

2. **WEST FACE   ★ 5.10+**
   Face and cracks with bolts. Protection to 3". FA: Dan Davis, Stan Shepard, 1961; FFA: Peter Croft, 1984.

3. **SOUTH FACE   5.11**
   Face and cracks with bolts. Protection to 1", bring keyhole hanger. FA: Fred Beckey, Dave Collins, 1957; FFA: Jim Yoder.

4. **NORTH FACE   5.5 A3**
   Cracks and face with bolts. Protection to 3". FA: Dan Davis and party, 1961.

Jupiter Rock

Waterfall Column

Drury Falls

JUPITER ROCK AND WATERFALL COLUMN

Two of the most inaccessible walls in the Leavenworth area, Jupiter Rock and Waterfall Column are also two of the largest. The approaches are horrendous (especially in winter), taking three hours at best, climbing gullies paralleling Drury Creek. Getting across the river is the hard part. Boating or wading are possibilities, but not recommended because of the risk of being washed down the river. Hiking from the Tumwater bridge upstream takes more time but is safer. Any way you go, it's going to take some time. Also plan on taking time to get back down and out. Don't think you can do it all in a day if you haven't been up there before. Be sure before you commit yourself.

Waterfall Column is obvious because of Drury Falls, a somewhat popular ice climb. The routes climb the cliff right of the falls. Descents are a decided ordeal. Either rappel the Original Route, involving at least two rappels and some difficult downclimbing, or descend a gully behind a buttress, then down a buttress to Jupiter Rock.

Descents from Jupiter Rock are also difficult, involving either downclimbing gullies or rappelling. On the whole, the climbs on these formations are, so far, not worth the hassles of approach and descent. There is much potential for new, long routes on these cliffs, however, awaiting a new breed of Washington pioneers.

WATERFALL COLUMN

1. **THE ORIGINAL ROUTE   III, 5.8**

    Originally, it was necessary to cross the falls after two pitches; now, there is a direct start on the right side of the falls. Climb cracks and chimneys to the top. Protection to 4". FA: Fred Beckey, John Parrott, Louis Pottschmidt, 1955.

2. **ENDGAME   IV, 5.9**

    Down from the Original start, on a terrace with a large roof, climb up seven pitches to the top. The fourth belay is on a ledge with spikes. A 5.8 pitch leads to a final 5.9 crack. Protection to 3". FA: Pete Doorish, Don Leonard, 1979.

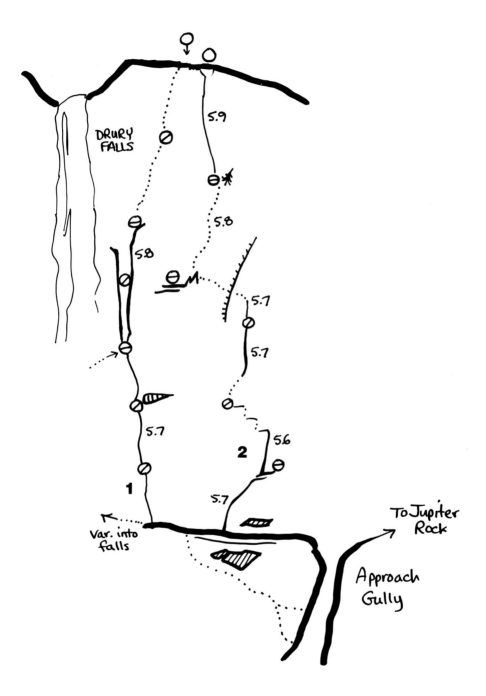

WATERFALL COLUMN

JUPITER ROCK

1. KING'S INDIAN   IV, 5.8
The route begins 70 yards uphill (left) from the lowest point of the cliff, following ramps and dihedrals to a roof. The fourth belay is on a large ledge. Skirt a roof to a major ledge system, then continue up the crux dihedral. At the end, tunnel through blocks to join **Nimzo Indian**. Protection to 3". FA: Pete Doorish, Don Leonard, 1979.

2. ZIG ZAG   III, 5.6
From the lowest point of the rock, follow a left-trending ledge system across **King's Indian**. Continue up a rib on the left skyline. Protection unknown. FA: Fred Beckey, Don Gordon, 1958.

3. NIMZO INDIAN   IV, 5.8
Just right of **Zig Zag's** start, climb up to a ledge with a pine tree. Easy climbing leads to a 5.8 face and a belay. Downclimb a short chimney then up past a flake and belay beside a large block. A short chimney leads to the main ledge system. Traverse right to an L-shaped pine tree, then climb 5.8 face and ramps to a bushy tree. Easy climbing leftward leads to another 5.8 section. Easy to the top. Eight pitches. Protection to 4". FA: Pete Doorish, Don Leonard, 1979.

4. DIRECT   III, 5.6 (not shown)
Scramble 200 yards right from **Zig Zag** and begin beside an obvious white wall. Climb to a ledge, then up a chimney and crack system to the top. Protection to 4". FA: Fred Beckey, Ed Cooper, Dave Collins, 1958.

5. FOUR KNIGHTS   III, 5.7 (not shown)
Climb **Direct** to where an easy traverse leads right to a large tree. Continue up and right through cracks, flakes and vegetation. Easier climbing higher up. Protection unknown. FA: Pete Doorish, Don Leonard, 1979.

SWIFTWATER

About two miles downstream from Tumwater campground is the Swiftwater picnic area. There are several boulders in this vicinity. Most of the problems are obvious. Royal Flush, a roof crack, is located across the road from the large black cave north of the parking lot.

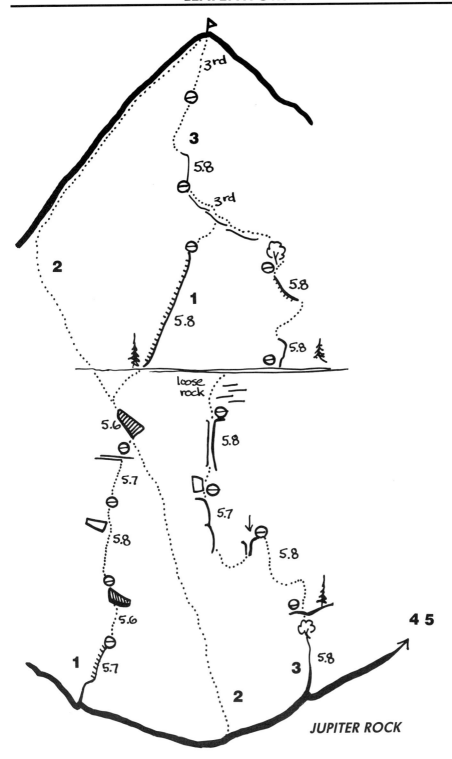

JUPITER ROCK

Nicola Masciandaro on the traverse pitch of Outer Space, Snow Creek Wall

ICICLE CREEK CANYON

The Icicle Creek Canyon is one of the major climbing areas in Washington, and probably the least well known. This is mainly because there has never been a published guide to the Icicle. This guide, while breaking that tradition, is not complete or comprehensive. It is a "bare bones" introduction to climbing in the Icicle, intended to give visiting climbers a way of finding some of the more or less obvious Icicle classics.

The canyon is located just west of Leavenworth. Drive up the Icicle River Road from the mouth of the Tumwater, heading south and then curving northwesterly into the canyon. There are numerous campgrounds in the Icicle, and most visiting climbers camp at Eightmile or Bridge Creek or else sack out on the ground of a parking lot or under a boulder. Camping is discouraged at any but clearly marked camping areas because private land ownership is making not only camping, but climbing, too, illegal in some places. There are many bivouac areas that are known to locals; if you need a place to camp and the campgrounds are full, ask around.

There is far more potential in the Icicle than this brief guide shows. If you are in an exploring mood, feel free to wander about and put up a "new" route. Just don't be surprised to find a fixed pin or rappel sling at the top.

Some will be upset that this guide includes the Icicle Creek Canyon. Others will be disappointed that more routes were not included. To the former, the author apologizes. However, in all fairness, with the closure of Peshastin Pinnacles to climbing, inclusion of the Icicle may help to spread climbers out. Additionally, with the closure of much land in the Icicle to private ownership and new housing construction, it was felt by many that now was the time to publish this guide. If climbing in the Icicle is to remain a legitimate activity, having a published guide, however incomplete, will be better than having no guide at all.

For those who wanted more, the author apologizes again. But seriously, it is unlikely that anyone alive knows every route in the Icicle by name, rating, and first ascent party, let alone someone who could map the whole of the canyon. If you really want to climb some obscure crack that no one has heard of, let alone climbed during the past 20 years, you will have to find it yourself. Come on, where's your spirit of adventure? (For those without a spirit of adventure, the next edition of this guide will likely have a more comprehensive guide to the Icicle.)

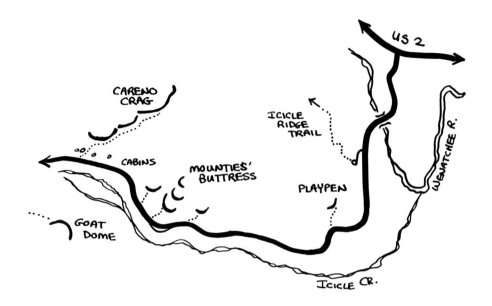

THE PLAYPEN

The Playpen is a small buttress hidden in the trees just before the road enters the canyon. About 200 yards from Camp Field is a road on the right. The cliff is up and right. Like too many of the other good, small crags in Icicle Creek Canyon, the Playpen is located on private property. It would be wise to ask permission before using the access.

1. **GREEN EGGS AND HAM   5.10c** (not shown)
   A double roof crack on the right. Beware of rope drag; double ropes recommended. Protection to 2″. FA: Jim Yoder, Lee Cunningham.
2. **D.A.M.M.   5.11c** (not shown)
   A conspicuous roof crack; the crux is turning the lip. Protection to 2″. FA: Dick Cilley, 1983.

MOUNTIES' BUTTRESS

This small series of stepped domes is one of Leavenworth's best and most-used instruction crags. It is located just downstream from the first cabins, about ½ mile before the Snow Creek parking lot. There are numerous short climbs to play on.

3. **LOWER BUTTRESS**
   The lower buttress has a number of crack climbs ranging from 5.0 to 5.7. There is some loose rock.
4. **MIDDLE OR FLAKE BUTTRESS   ★★★**
   Flake Buttress has two excellent crack climbs on the left (5.6), and an easier righthand route.
5. **DISH CRACK   5.10c (PG-13)** (not shown)
   A thin crack in a bowl on the formation about 100 yards left across the gully from Mountie's Buttress. Usually toproped. Protection to ¾″; include TCUs. FA: unknown.

MOUNTIES' BUTTRESS

GOAT DOME

The broad dome directly across Icicle Creek from Mounties' Buttress. Access is via the Snow Lakes Trail. At end of the leftmost switchback, take a faint trail eastward. The trail leads to Sunrise Crack.

6. **SUNRISE CRACK** ★ **5.10c**
   Thin crack through roof. Protection to 2″. FA: Mike Jakubal, 1982.
7. **UNKNOWN ENTITY** ★ **5.9**
   Long dihedral groove system on north side, visible from the road. Protection to 2″. FA: unknown.

GOAT DOME

CARENO CRAG

Careno Crag is one of the premier crags in the Icicle. It has a growing number of excellent crack climbs, and is complimented with a few difficult face routes. Early Morning Overhang, a huge roof visible above the road, is at the lower end of the formation. There are numerous routes and possibilities farther uphill.

8. **RIDE OF THE VALKYRIES (aka EARLY MORNING OVERHANG)**   ★ **5.12a** (not shown)
   Obvious roof above A-frame cabins. First pitch is 5.7. Approach to the roof has loose blocks. Protection to 2½″. FFA: Hugh Herr, 1986.

The following routes are arranged as one walks uphill from Ride of the Valkyries.

9. **BLACK POWER**   ★ **5.11+**
   A prominent bolted arete a distance uphill from the Early Morning Overhang. FA: Greg Child, Greg Collum 1984.

10. **CARENO CRAG**   ★★ **5.10a**
    This route begins with an angling thin crack, which reaches the prominent central dihedral system. Four pitches. The final pitch stays right of the actual corner. Protection unknown. FA: Fred Beckey. Variation 1: From the first belay of the Careno Crag route, climb the righthand face/arete (5.9, PG-13). Bolts, but bring protection to 1½″. Variation 2: From the second belay in the dihedral, climb the obvious righthand flake to the face/arete (5.11b/c). Bolts, but bring protection to 2½″ for the flake.

11. **M.J.B. ARETE**   ★ **5.11a/b**
    A bolted arete right of the dihedrals. FA: Matt Kerns, Jim Yoder, Bill Crawford 1986.

12. **M.J.B. TOWER**   ★ **5.9**
    Cracks lead to this esteemed summit. Protection to 2″. FA: Matt Kerns, Jim Yoder, Bill Crawford 1986.

13. **PUMPLINE**   ★★ **5.10d/11a**
    A prominent crack right of the M.J.B. routes. Protection to 2″, with RPs suggested. FA: Unknown.

14. **FREE FLOYD**   **5.10a/b**
    A thin crack right of Pumpline. Small wired nuts. FA: Jim Yoder, Tim Wilson.

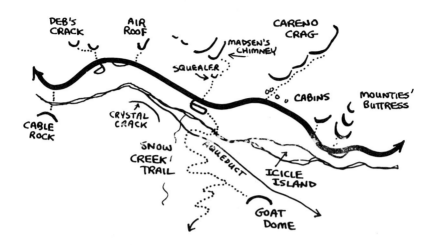

SNOW CREEK PARKING LOT

There are numerous toprope and lead cracks in the vicinity of the Snow Creek parking lot and along the road up canyon. Boulder problems abound in this area, especially near Bolt Rock.

15. **THE PROW** ★★ **5.11+ (TR)**
Overhanging face climb on Bolt Rock, on the right side of the road just before the parking lot. FA: Erik Thixton, 1976.

16. **SQUEALER (aka EAST OF JAVA)** c **5.12a** (not shown)
Short, overhanging finger crack directly across the road and up hill from the parking lot. FA: Dick Cilley (TR), 1982; FLA: Jeff Smoot (solo), 1986.

17. **LA CUCARACHA** ★ **5.10b** (not shown)
Steep thin crack uphill from Squealer. Toprope or lead. Protection to 1½". FA: unknown.

18. **MADSEN'S CHIMNEY** **5.9/10** (not shown)
Obvious offwidth/chimney right of La Cucaracha. FA: Jim Madsen.

19. **AIR ROOF** ★★★ **5.11b** (not shown)
Roof crack pitch hidden in trees up road from parking lot, on right. Protection to 2". FA: Cal Folsom, 1978.

20. **WILLIAMS' TWELVE (aka NIGHTMARE ON FRONT STREET)** ★★ **5.12a (PG-13)**
Obvious slanting fingertip crack above road on right, 200 yards up road from Snow Creek parking lot. Usually toproped, but has been led. Protection to ¾", including camming units. FA: Bob Williams (TR); FLA: Jeff Smoot, 1987.

21. **DEB'S CRACK** ★★★ **5.10c**
Overhanging, left-slanting crack above Williams' Twelve. Infrequently led. Protection to 2". FA: unknown.

22. **ZIG ZAG** **5.11+ (TR)**
Dihedral left of Deb's Crack. FA: Matt Christiansen.

23. **CRYSTAL CRACK** **5.8** (not shown)
A unique crack which has formed beside a crystal dike in the small dome above and right of the aqueduct bridge, across the river from the road. Protection unknown. FA: unknown.

BOLT ROCK – THE PROW

WILLIAMS' TWELVE

DEB'S CRACK/ZIG ZAG

CABLE ROCK

About ½ mile upstream from Snow Creek parking lot is this small, slabby face across the creek. Access is via a cable, or a long, brushy hike from Snow Creek Trail. There are several routes in the 5.7 to 5.10 range, most of which were cleaned once, but which have since become somewhat mossy or dirty as they see few ascents, and because of seepage.

24. **CABLE CRACK**   **5.7** (not shown)

The central crack system. Frequently wet. Protection to 2". FA: unknown.

BRUCE'S BOULDER

The squat dome on left side of road at about the six mile mark. Bruce's Boulder has many popular toprope friction problems. This area is frequently used for beginning instruction courses.

25. **RIVER FACE**   ★ **5.11a (TR)** (not shown)

The obvious face climb on the river face of the boulder. FA: unknown.

Across the road from Bruce's Boulder is a slabby wall with numerous cracks and friction problems, ranging from 5.6 to 5.11.

26. **A SLICE OF PIE**   ★ **5.11a** (not shown)

Hidden toprope problem across the road from Bruce's Boulder, behind a large flake. FA: Dick Cilley, 1982.

MUSCLE BEACH

A buttress hanging over a deep pool in the creek between Bruce's Boulder and Z-Crack Buttress. A hard-to-find trail leads through brush about 200 yards down the road from Z-Crack Buttress to the creek. A popular swimming hole, with three routes, which are easily and best toproped.

27. **TITTIES & BEER   5.10c** (not shown)
    Traverse left to farthest, widest crack finish. Protection to 2". FA: unknown.
28. **MUSCLE BEACH   ★ 5.11a** (not shown)
    The middle crack. Protection to 1". FA: Dick Cilley, 1982. Direct start 5.10d (toprope).
29. **GOLD'S GYM   ★ 5.11b/c (PG-13)** (not shown)
    The righthand crack/seam. Protection to ½"; difficult to place. FA: Dick Cilley, 1982.

RAT CREEK BOULDER

A large isolated boulder across the creek, up the road from Bruce's Boulder. Access is via the bridge on left side of the road. Unfortunately, this is now on private property, and signs are posted. The boulder is mis-named; it is nearer to Hook Creek.

30. **ARCH   ★★★ 5.10c (TR)** (not shown)
    Prominent arch in the middle of the hidden face of the boulder. FA: Jim Madsen.

Upstream from "Rat Creek Boulder" are two distinct crags – Hook Creek Crag and Rat Creek Dome. Hook Creek Crag is somewhat inobvious, but has a few worthwhile routes and more cleaning projects. It can most easily be reached by hiking up beside Hook Creek.

Rat Creek Dome, a broad shield on the crest between the Hook and Rat Creek drainages, has many steep cracks and roofs. Below, among the many large boulders beside Rat Creek, is Atlas Shrugged, and several other short toprope and lead routes.

Sadly, the access road to all this climbing is privately owned. Climbers wishing to visit these crags must either ask permission or rig a tyrolean across from Icicle Buttress – or else pass unnoticed. A low profile here is definitely in order.

31. **BROOM CRACK   ★ 5.10b** (not shown)
    On the far left side of Rat Creek Dome is this double crack, set just left of the main formation. Protection to 1". FA: Doug Klewin, Dan McNerthney, 1979.
32. **CLEAN SWEEP   5.11b (TR)** (not shown)
    Right of Broom Crack, on the main cliff, is a short, overhanging thin crack. FA: Dick Cilley, 1983.
33. **BRUSH WITH DEATH   5.9+** (not shown)
    A roof route high on the center of the crag. Approach via 5.7 cracks on the left. Protection to 3". FA: Mike Jakubal, Dick Cilley, 1983.
34. **FLAKE   ★ 5.11b (R)** (not shown)
    A wafer-flake lieback on the right side of the cliff leads to unprotected face and thin cracks on a slab. Protection to 1½"; take care not to destroy the flake. FA: Mike Jakubal, 1984.
35. **ATLAS SHRUGGED   ★★★ 5.11d** (not shown)
    Excellent overhanging crack on the "real" Rat Creek boulder. Take the road up river about ½ mile from Rat Creek boulder. FA: Dick Cilley, 1982.
36. **BABY'S ON FIRE   5.13a (TR)** (not shown)
    Thin crack left of Atlas Shrugged. FA: Max Dufford.

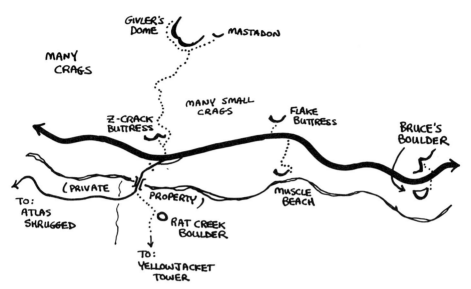

Z-CRACK BUTTRESS

A small crag beside the road, across the road from the access road to Rat Creek Boulder, with three obvious crack lines.

37. **Z-CRACK** ★★ **5.10b**
Cracks on left face of crag, starting with a small roof. Protection to 2". FA: Jim Madsen.

38. **ALCOVE CRACK** ★★ **5.9**
Wide cracks in the middle of the crag, with a small roof at mid-height. Protection to 3". FA: unknown.

39. **A-CRACK** ★★ **5.8**
Righthand crack, slightly recessed. Starts thin, to hand size. Face variation to start. Protection to 2". FA: unknown.

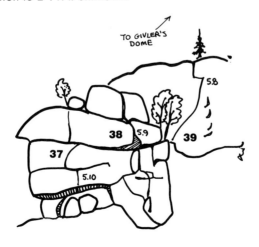

Z-CRACK BUTTRESS

GIVLER'S DOME

The obvious dome high above the road at Z-Crack Buttress, its most prominent feature being a hand crack near the middle. A trail begins on right side of Z-Crack Buttress. There are many short routes along or near the trail in either direction, including numerous routes on the slabs and cliffs right of the trail ranging from 5.6 to 5.11. This is a fun area to explore.

40. **GIVLER'S DOME** ★★★ **5.7**
    A one or two pitch crack splitting the dome. Short face at start. Direct start crack is 5.8. Protection to 2". FA: John Marts.

41. **TIMSON'S FACE ROUTE** ★★ **5.10c**
    Tuolumne-style face climb replete with runouts, right of crack. Fixed protection. FA: Pat Timson. Note: There are purportedly two such routes. However, the climb described is the most obvious. The other apparently winds its way between the crack route and the more obvious face pitch on the right, and is rated 5.10. FA: Pat Timson.

42. **QUAALUDES AND RED WINE** **5.10b** (not shown)
    Face climb right of Timson's route. Bring #2½ Friend. FA: Tim Wilson, Jim Yoder, 1984.

43. **MASTADON** ★ **5.11c** (not shown)
    Obvious large roof on the separate crag a short walk right of Givler's Dome. Protection to 4". FA: Dan Lepeska, Dick Cilley, 1982.

44. **THE BARFING HOOF** **5.10a (X)**
    Take the dished face left of Givler's Dome belay. Bent bolts, death runouts. Protection imaginary. FA: Doug Klewin, Pat McNerthney, 1979.

45. **DIRECT START FLAKE** **5.10c**
    A direct start to Barfing Hoof, taking a wide, thin flake on the left. Protection to 4"(?). FA: unknown.

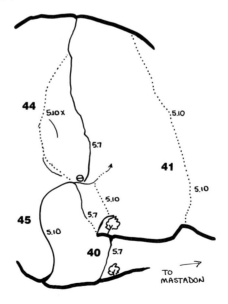

GIVLER'S DOME

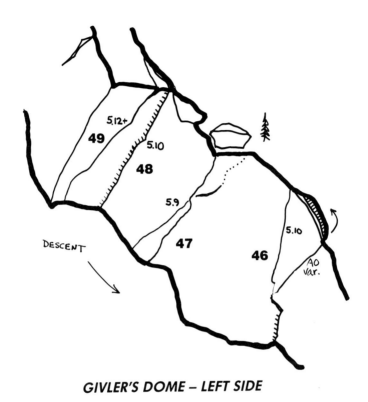

GIVLER'S DOME – LEFT SIDE

46. **BO DEREK** ★★★ **5.10b**
Stunning steep flake on upper left flank of Givler's Dome. Protection to 1½". FA: Dan McNerthney, Dean Geiselman, 1980.

47. **THE ENEMA** **5.9+**
Crack/seam on outside corner/slab on far upper left flank. Protection to 1½". FA: Jim Yoder, Pat McNerthney, 1979.

48. **BONDAGE** ★ **5.10c**
Wickedly leaning corner crack left of the Enema. Protection to 3". FA: Doug Klewin, 1979.

49. **NEVER-NEVER** ★ **5.12d**
Amazing roof crack left of **Bondage**. Can't miss it. Protection to 2½". FA: Todd Skinner, 1983.

The area between Givler's Dome and Icicle Buttress has much of the unexplored wealth of the Icicle. Obvious crags abound here, including Eagle Rock and Peek-a-boo Tower, with numerous uncharted cracks, slabs and roofs. However, few climbers – this author included – have climbed here, and fewer still know the names or ratings of more than a handful of routes. For those who feel the Icicle has been destroyed by inclusion in this guide, they can at least find solace in this area – and others farther up the canyon.

ICICLE BUTTRESS — LEFT

ICICLE BUTTRESS
Large formation 100-yards up road from Z-Crack, on right. Has several prominent corners and roofs. Numerous possibilities. Several 5.11 or harder routes, and also abundant 5.7-5.9 routes.

50. **COCAINE CRACK**   ⋆⋆ **5.10a**
Thin crack splitting a slab on the upper left side. Scramble to base. Protection to 1½". FA: Del Young, Catherine Freer.

51. **BIG BERTHA**   ⋆ **5.11d**
Huge roof above and right from Cocaine Crack. Protection to 4". FA: Jim Yoder, 1984.

52. **JOHN HENRY**   **5.11a**
A roof route left of, and down the ramp from Big Bertha. Protection to 3". FA: Lee Cunningham, 1984.

53. **VICE GRIP**   **5.11c**
Right about 150 feet and level with the start of Cocaine Crack is a short wall with two overhanging cracks. This is the the left-most crack/face line. Protection to 1½". FA: unknown.

54. **SPECKLED GUMS**   ⋆ **5.10a**
Just off the road, below Fork Crack, this route is a crack through two short overhangs, just right of a prominent prow. Protection to 2". FA: Jim Yoder.

55. **PROTEUS**   ⋆ **5.11b**
Right of Speckled Gums, a short face reaches a ramp and crack. Protection to 2". FA: Alison Osius, Mike Jakubal, 1982.

56. **FORK CRACK**   **5.9**
Obvious forked crack on lower right section of crag. Protection to 2½". FA: unknown.

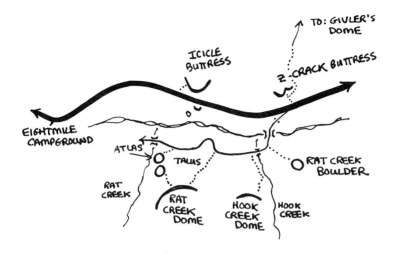

ICICLE BUTTRESS – RIGHT

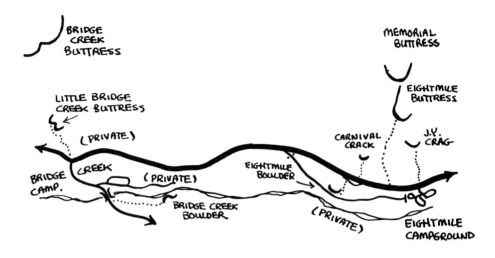

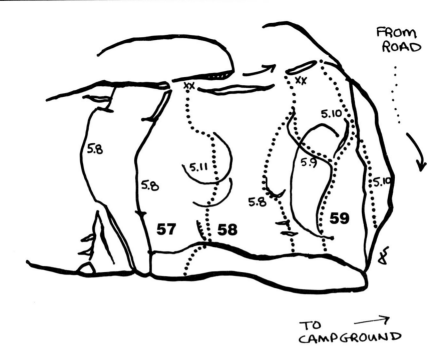

EIGHTMILE BOULDER

A popular cliff just up the road from Eightmile Campground. May park in camp and walk up access road or descend from main road. Located on private property, so be respectful of owner's rights. Most routes are best toproped, although most may be led.

57. **CLASSIC CRACK** ★★★ **5.8**
   Central, textbook handcrack. Top-roped, led and soloed regularly. FA: unknown.

58. **DOIN' DISHES** **5.11d (TR)**
   Thin face climb up depressions right of Classic Crack. FA: Dick Cilley, 1982.

59. **DECEPTION** **5.9+**
   Slanting crack on right side of cliff which looks pretty easy. FA: unknown.

60. **CARNIVAL CRACK** **5.10c**
   Steep offwidth across the road from Eightmile Boulder. FA: unknown.

Above Eightmile Campground lies an expanse of large rock formations, including the vast, largely unexplored Bridge Creek and Memorial Buttresses. Route development on these crags is in its infancy, although a number of multi-pitch routes have been climbed. This guide will, for now, pretend this area does not exist, hopefully preserving the balance for those who wish that no guide to any of the Icicle was included in this book.

61. **EIGHTMILE BUTTRESS** ★ **III, 5.6 or 5.7**
   This is the lowest buttress above Eightmile Campground. A faint path leads to the crag from about 100 yards up the road from the entrance to the campground. The route is most easily identified by a wide, white crack 200 feet above the ground. The first pitch takes either an unprotected chimney (5.6), or a steep crack on the right (5.7). From above the white crack, stray rightward up ramps. Seven pitches to easy descent. Merges with Memorial Buttress. Protection to 4". FA: unknown.

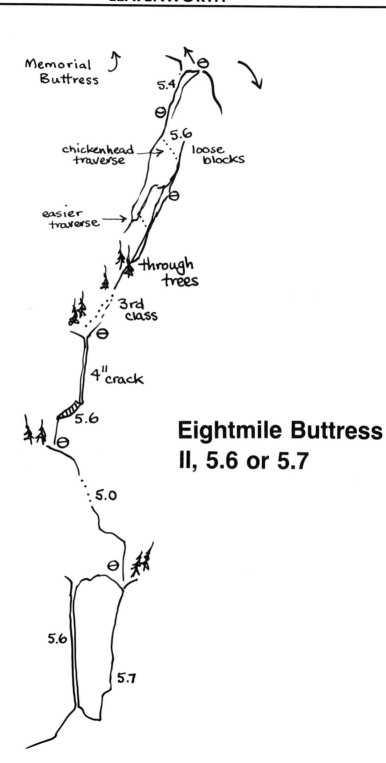

Memorial Buttress

5.4

5.6

chickenhead traverse

loose blocks

easier traverse

through trees

3rd class

4" crack

5.6

5.0

5.6

5.7

**Eightmile Buttress
II, 5.6 or 5.7**

Nicola Masciandaro on an unnamed slab at Little Bridge Creek Buttress

DOCTOR ROCK

Doctor Rock is the small dome across the river from and higher up than Eightmile Boulder. Access crosses private property. Again, it is best to ask permission first. Doctor Rock has one notable route, a 5.11 thin lieback.

BRIDGE CREEK BOULDER

Just across Icicle Creek from Bridge Creek Campground is a small buttress with two notable routes. Access is via a trail leading downstream from the south end of the bridge.

62. **KITTEN WITH A WHIP**   **5.11a/b (TR)** (not shown)
    On the left, climb a blocky wall to a thin roof crack. Could be led. Loose blocks. FA: Dick Cilley, Jeff Smoot, 1984.

63. **LITTLE RED CORVETTE**   **5.11d (TR)** (not shown)
    Thin crack rising straight out of the creek. During low water, a boulder provides a platform. FA: Dick Cilley, 1984.

LITTLE BRIDGE CREEK BUTTRESS

Little Bridge Creek Buttress is a small, hidden bluff across the road from the entrance to Bridge Creek Campground. A trail leads up and left from the road, across private property, about 200 yards to the cliff. All routes are about 50 to 75 feet long, and may be descended by walking off the upper left side by a rude path.

64. **DISHONORABLE DISCHARGE**   ★ **5.10b**
    On the far left side of the buttress is this short, overhanging finger crack leading through a wide flare. Protection to 1″. FA: Brent Hoffman, Gary Jones.

65. **CONSCIENTIOUS OBJECTOR**   **5.10a (X)**
    Right of Discharge is a vertical or over-vertical seam leading to several large, blocky face holds. No protection for 30 feet. FA: Brent Hoffman, Gary Jones. Variation: The shallow seam between Discharge and Objector; a "direct" start to the latter (5.11b). FA: Jeff Smoot, Marc Twight (TR).

66. **ARMS CONTROL**   ★ **5.9+ or 5.10a**
    Right, around the arete from the previous routes, is this steep, thin crack/flake/ face route. Protection to 2″. FA: Brent Hoffman, Gary Jones.

67. **CORNER**   **5.5**
    The obvious, wide dihedral right of Arms Control. Climb face crack into easy dihedral. Protection to 1″. FA: Brent Hoffman, Gary Jones.

68. **SLAB**   **5.7 (X)**
    Climb the long slab directly above the previously mentioned face crack. Protection illusory. May be toproped. FA: unknown.

69. **ARETE**   **5.8 (X)**
    The blunt arete/face pitch right of the slab. No protection. May be toproped. FA: unknown.

70. **SEAM**   **rating unknown** (not shown)
    The obvious, thin, overhanging seam on the right-most portion of the cliff. It has been aided, but has resisted all free climbing attempts. FA: unknown.

THE EGG

The Egg is a very large boulder just off the road about one-half mile upcanyon from Bridge Creek Campground, on the right. It has a 5.11 toprope problem (FA: Jim Yoder).

FOURTH-OF-JULY BUTTRESS

This small cliff has several routes. It is in the vicinity of the Fourth-of-July trailhead.

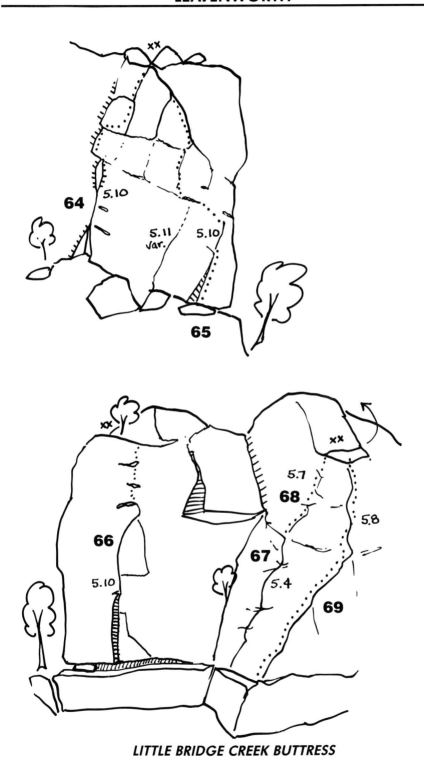

LITTLE BRIDGE CREEK BUTTRESS

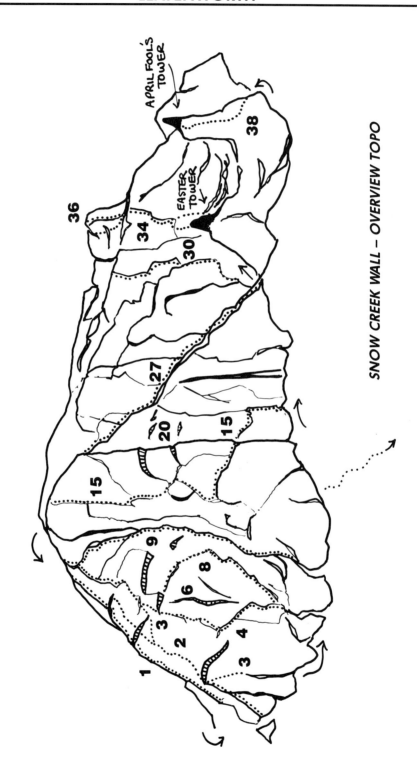

SNOW CREEK WALL – OVERVIEW TOPO

SNOW CREEK WALL

The Snow Creek Wall is the largest climbing wall in Leavenworth, outside of the mountains. Located above Icicle Creek Canyon, the cliff is reached by a two mile hike up the Snow Creek Trail. The trail starts at the obvious large parking lot about four miles up the Icicle River Road from Leavenworth, and it is steep, switchbacking relentlessly for almost one mile before leveling off. When directly across the canyon from the wall, a path drops down to the creek and a log crossing, then up the dusty opposite wall to the base of the cliff, directly below Two Trees Ledge. Hiking time to the wall is about 45 minutes. Start early to beat the heat and the crowds. Camping is available beside the creek for those who want to carry all that stuff up from the car.

Beware of leaving valuables visible in your car at the parking lot. There have been many ripoffs, even in broad daylight. Don't tempt would-be thieves – put your stuff in the trunk.

Descents from the wall are complex. The simplest is to walk off the left side. This involves downclimbing sandy ledges and following a faint trail. The trail eventually skirts the left side of the cliff, but may require rappelling if you don't get on the right path. It is also possible to rappel down the right side of the cliff, but this is more complex and not recommended.

The routes tend to be five to seven pitches in length, mostly in crack systems or climbing knobby slabs. Some routes are very serious in nature, with little or no protection, while others are "safe" and enjoyable. As with any "big wall", be prepared for anything.

1. **SATELLITE** ★ II, 5.7
   At the left end of the wall is an obvious right-facing corner; climb cracks on the left to tree and continue up cracks on right through roof. Five pitches. Protection to 1". FA: Fred Beckey, Steve Marts, 1963; FFA: Tacoma party.
2. **CHTON** III, 5.9+ (PG-13)
   Beginning in a hole near the left end of a long roof; climb up cracks and through roofs. Six pitches. Protection to 2". FA: Jim McCarthey, Jim Wilcox.
3. **LOST PLANET AIRMEN** III, 5.9
   Variation which joins Chton for three pitches then heads off right to cross Orbit. Six pitches. Protection to 2". FA: Craig Cutler, Mike Heil, 1980.
4. **ORBIT** ★★★ III, 5.8 (R)
   Climb chimney to base of Mary Jane Dihedral, then traverse left under long roof to dihedral. Face climb higher through roof. Seven pitches. Some long runouts. Protection to 3"; include small wired nuts. FA: Fred Beckey, Dan Davis, 1962; FFA: Ron Burgner, John Marts, 1966.
5. **BLAST OFF** ★ 5.10
   Dihedral variation of first pitch of Orbit, on the left. Meets Orbit at second pitch. Protection to 2". FA: Dave Carmen, 1969.
6. **MARY JANE DIHEDRAL** ★★ III, 5.9
   Obvious two pitch dihedral right of Orbit. Some face climbing. Joins Orbit at large roof. Seven pitches total. Protection to 2". FA: Don McPherson, Ron Burgner, Jim Madsen.

7. **CARLA'S TRAVERSE** 5.10a (R)
Traverse from near the middle of Mary Jane Dihedral leftward to join Orbit below its third belay. Marginal protection. FA: Carla Firey.

8. **CHIMNEY SWEEP** III, 5.10b
From below chimney on first pitch of Orbit/Mary Jane Dihedral, head off right. Climb rightward up face and chimney, then back left to join Orbit at roof. Seven pitches. Protection to 2". FA: Al Givler, Jim Langdon, 1970.

9. **GALAXY** IV, 5.8+
Long route climbing obvious brushy corner system on middle left side. Starts from top of small white slab. Little routefinding difficulty. Nine pitches. Protection to 3". FA: Pat Callis, Bob Phelps, 1964; FFA: Jim Madsen, Tom Hargis, Don McPherson, Dan Davis.

10. **WALTZ** III 5.8+
Variation to Galaxy. From 4th belay, head left across cracks to crooked tree. Joins Orbit. FA: Any of a dozen climbers between 1970 and 1978.

11. **HYPERSPACE** ★★★ II, 5.10d
Use Galaxy or Iconoclast to reach this finish variation, taking a wild chimney/corner through the final overhangs above Galaxy. Two pitches. Protection to 3". FA: Jim Yoder, Neil Cannon, Kevin Buselmeier, 1983.

12. **JET STREAM DELIVERY** ★ III, 5.10d
From the first belay on Galaxy, climb rightward (to bolt) and up to Iconoclast. Climb thin crack on right (meets Iconoclast), then left and up to a bush. Continue rightward, then up a dihedral paralleling Iconoclast on its left. From large blocks at the dihedral's end, face traverse right to meet Iconoclast. Protection to 3", including many small and medium (RPs and TCUs helpful). FA: Brian Burdo, Pete Doorish, Greg White, 1988.

13. **ICONOCLAST** ★★★ III, 5.11b or 5.12
Excellent route starting on slabs just above dead log at trail's end. Climb any variation to a ledge with a tree, then face climb past roofs to blocky ledge. Continue up and rightward in dihedrals, passing overhangs, to reach Library Ledge (5.10). Final two pitches can be avoided by finishing via Outer Space. Six pitches. Protection to 3". FA: Mead Hargis, Tom Hargis, 1971 (to Library Ledge); FFA: Pat McNerthney, 1984 (left variation finish); Jim Yoder, Bob Plum, 1985 (direct).

14. **EDGE OF SPACE** ★★★ 5.11c
Two pitch variation finish of Iconoclast, taking face to the arete of the Galaxy dihedral system. Fixed protection. Two pitches. FA: Pat McNerthney, David Rubine, 1985.

15. **OUTER SPACE** ★★★ III, 5.9
The classic Snow Creek Wall outing. Starts in a dihedral just left of White Slabs, then traverses left to Two Trees Ledge. Crux traverse crack leads rightward to face pitch, then two spectacular pitches up face crack to top. Seven pitches. Protection to 2½"; 165-foot rope helpful. FA: Fred Beckey, Ron Niccoli, 1960; FFA: Fred Beckey, Steve Marts, 1963.

16. **R.P.M.** III, 5.10d (X)
An intertwining variation of Outer Space which starts with a difficult slab pitch (crux), eventually reaching Two Trees Ledge via one of several variations. Face climb left of Outer Space traverse, then parallel the crack pitches on the right. Seven pitches. Protection marginal; full-pitch runouts; protection to 2", including tie-off loops for chickenheads. FA: Pat Timson, Steve Graupe, Rick LeDuc, 1975.

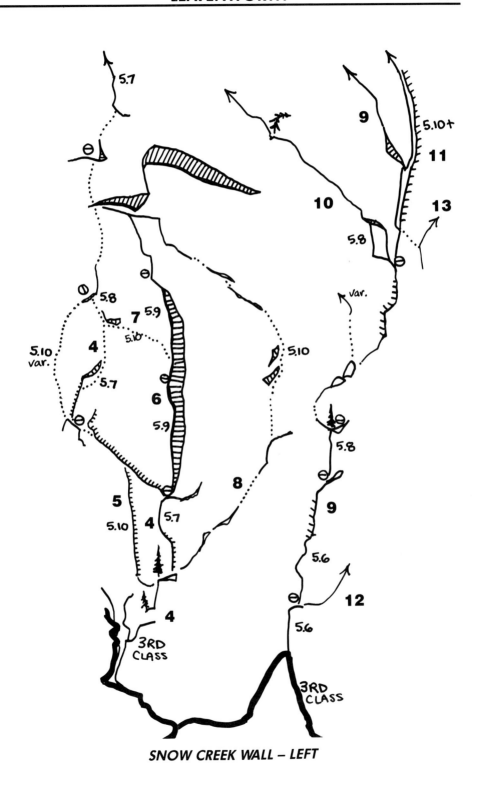

SNOW CREEK WALL – LEFT

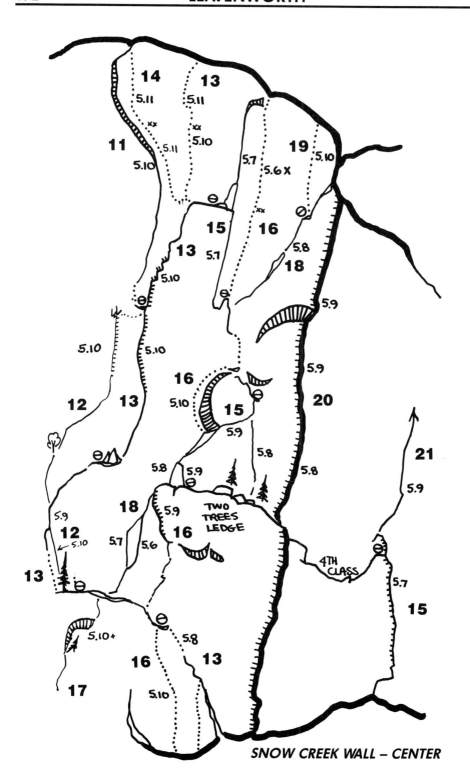

SNOW CREEK WALL – CENTER

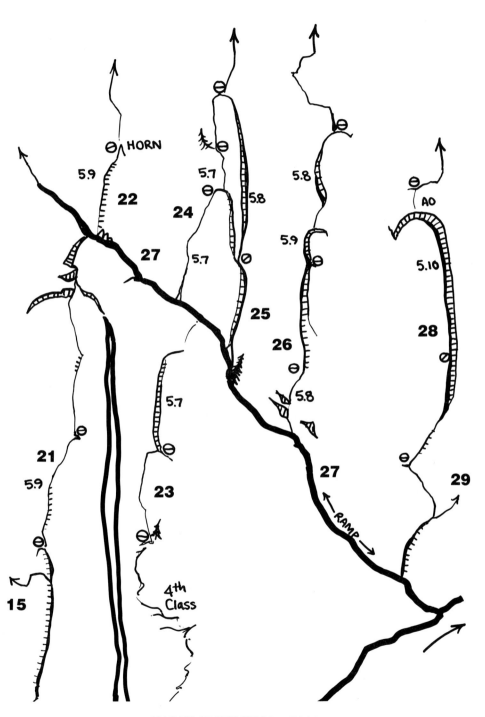

SNOW CREEK WALL – RIGHT

17. **SLINGSHOT   5.10d**
Variation approach pitch for Iconoclast, left of R.P.M. start. Climbs through cleaned roof using a tree as a catapult, or some such nonsense. Protection to 3". FA: Jim Yoder, Lee Cunningham, 1984.

18. **REMORSE   III, 5.8 (R)**
Starting directly below Two Trees Ledge, a dirty ledge gains a 5.8 traverse left to a broad ledge. Traverse right (5.6 or 5.9) to gain Two Trees Ledge. Halfway across, climb steep cracks to join Outer Space at end of traverse pitch. From below pedestal, traverse rightward on chickenheads and shelves for two pitches to meet Northern Dihedral. Seven pitches. Marginal protection to 3". FA: Ed Cooper, Galen McBee, 1958; FFA: Ron Burgner, Don McPherson.

19. **REGRESSION   5.10a (R/X)**
From the last belay on Remorse, climb straight up past bolt. One pitch. Marginal, unknown protection; possibly one bolt. FA: Bob Crawford.

20. **NORTHERN DIHEDRAL   III, 5.9**
The obvious long dihedral right of Outer Space. Little routefinding difficulty. Blocky and mossy. Six pitches. Protection to 2". FA: Jim Stuart, Alex Bertulis, 1964; FFA: Jim Madsen, Ron Burgner, 1967.

21. **WHITE SLABS DIRECT   II, 5.9**
Continue straight up first dihedral of Outer Space for three more pitches. Protection to 2½". FA: Jim Madsen, Don McPherson.

22. **WHITE FRIGHT   ★ II, 5.9+**
An obvious corner just right of where White Slabs Direct meets Country Club ramp. Two pitches up corner and cracks. Belay at horn. Protection to 2". FA: Fred Beckey, Charles Bell, 1961; FFA: Jim Madsen, Phil Leatherman.

23. **WHITE SLABS   ★ II, 5.7**
Scrambling to a tree right of obvious water streaks leads to a long pitch, then an obvious corner. Can rappel down ramp or finish via any variation. Four pitches. Protection to 2". FA: Don Gordon, John Rupley, 1958; FFA: Fred Beckey, Charles Bell, 1961.

24. **UMBRELLA TREE   II, 5.7**
Continue from where White Slabs meets Country Club via face climbing to the Umbrella Tree. Can continue up chimney system, although many rappel from tree. Five pitches. Protection to 1". FA: Fred Beckey, Pat Callis, 1963.

25. **KING KONG   II, 5.8**
Right of Umbrella Tree, starting above a large tree, is this blocky chimney system. It is the lefthand chimney. Five pitches. Protection to 3". FA: Don Gordon, John Rupley, 1959; FFA: Rich Doorish.

26. **TEMPEST   II, 5.9+**
A chimney system right of King Kong. The final pitches are Class 4. Five pitches. Protection to 2". FA: Ed Cooper, Jack Miller, 1959; FFA: Fred Beckey, Pete Williamson, 1968.

27. **COUNTRY CLUB   (−★) II, 5.4**
A trashy ramp system that is better used to connect routes than as an actual route. Protection unknown. FA: Fred Beckey, Don Gordon, 1958.

28. **GRAND ARCH   ★ II, 5.10 A0**
Climb rightward from base of Country Club to reach clean, left-curving arch. Move out of arch may go free. Protection to 2". FA: Fred Beckey, Steve Marts, 1963; FFA: Mark Weigelt, Mead Hargis (except aid point), 1970.

29. HALLOWEEN BUTTRESS   II, 5.9+
A mysterious route that no one seems to know much about. *Washington Rock* described it as "largely unknown climbing." It still is. Climb several pitches right of Grand Arch. Protection unknown. FA: Fred Beckey, Eric Bjørnstad, 1967; FFA: Pete Doorish, Don Leonard.

30. NAILWAY   II, 5.9+ (?)
An obvious, left-facing corner left of Champagne. The rating has not been confirmed. May be aid. Protection to 2". FA: Steve Marts, Dan Davis, Jerry Feucht, 1963; FFA: unknown.

31. EASTER TOWER, NOTCH   ★ 5.7 (not shown)
Scramble to the notch via Class 3 and 4. Climb obvious cracks. Protection to 1". FA: Tim Kelley, Art Maki; FFA: Fred Beckey, 1966.

32. EASTER TOWER, NORTH FACE   (−★) 5.8 (not shown)
Somewhat rotten cracks on the north face. Protection to 2". FA: unknown.

33. EASTER TOWER, OUTSIDE FACE   rating unknown. (not shown)
Involves several pitches of aid. FA: unknown.

34. CHAMPAGNE   ★ II, 5.7
From the notch of Easter Tower, climb flakes, cracks and corners bearing rightward. Protection to 2½". FA: Steve Marts, Bill Marts, Jerry Feucht, 1963; FFA: Fred Beckey, Pat Callis.

35. SPRING FEVER   ★ 5.8 (not shown)
Climb face and cracks right of Champagne. Connects with Champagne at ledges. Protection to 2". FA: Fred Beckey, Bill Marts, 1964; FFA: Beckey, 1966.

36. CHICKEN ON A LEASH   ★ 5.10c
An obvious white corner near Spring Fever's end, high on the wall. Protection to 2". FA: Rich Carlstad, Dave Anderson, 1980.

37. APRIL FOOL'S TOWER   ★ 5.8
From notch, traverse across north ledges and climb outside face cracks. Protection to 2". FA: Fred Beckey (by inside corner); FA: Dick Berge and party (by route described).

38. TARKUS   5.9
Direct cracks leading to ledge at outside face of April Fool's Tower. Protection to 3". FA: Mead Hargis.

39. VICIOUS RUMOR   ★★ 5.11a (not shown)
A short, overhanging crack near the base of April Fool's Tower. Protection to 2". FA: Dave Anderson, Rich Carlstad, 1980.

40. OVERHANG CORNER   5.9+ (not shown)
An overhanging dihedral crack on the south side of April Fool's Tower. Can be reached by scrambling or by rappel. Protection to 4". FA: Mead Hargis, Bruce Albert, 1970.

41. RIVER GUANGE   5.6 (not shown)
As reported in *Washington Rock,* cracks and knobs seen from Vicious Rumor. Protection unknown. FA: Rich Carlstad, Dave Anderson, 1980.

42. GUIARDIA BUTTRESS   5.8 (not shown)
As reported in *Washington Rock,* two pitches which may be seen from Icicle Road. Protection unknown. FA: Rich Carlstad, Dave Anderson, 1980.

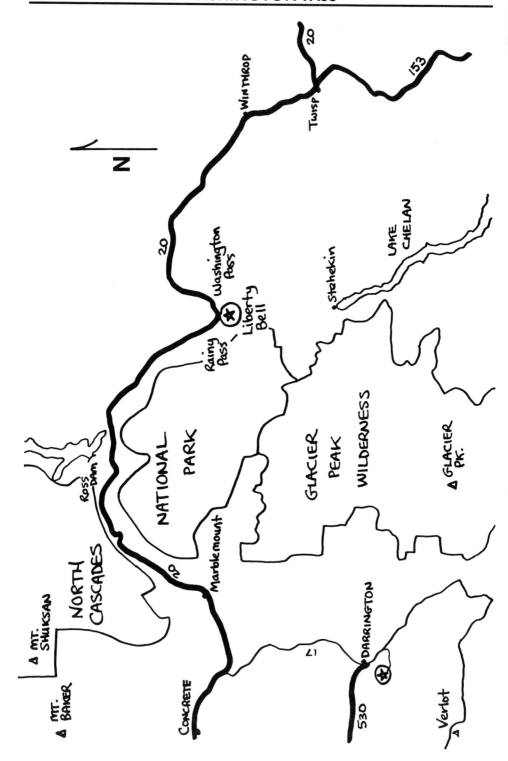

WASHINGTON PASS

It is with some trepidation that the author includes this section of the guide. There is little doubt that the climbs of Liberty Bell and the Early Winter Spires are of interest to rock climbers; however, because these are mountain routes, subject to mountain weather, with snow on approaches and descents, and a more serious level of commitment, this area lies at the fringe of the intended scope of this guide.

Nevertheless, this fine area will be presented here, because its roadside location and superb climbing combine to lure visitors from the more casual lowland climbing areas. The better quality, pure alpine rock routes will receive more detailed discussion, while the gully and couloir routes, and routes with poor rock or unaesthetic climbing, will be discussed cursorily, if at all, usually only when they are used as landmarks or descents.

The routes detailed in this section are all located on the Liberty Bell massif, consisting of the namesake Liberty Bell (7720'), and continuing south along a jagged crest with Concord Tower (7560') and Lexington Tower (7560'), and the more pronounced North (7760') and South (7807') Early Winter Spires.

This cluster of peaks offers an impressive assortment of alpine rock climbs, from the "easy" **Beckey Route** on Liberty Bell (5.6) to the aid horrors of **Midnight Ride** on South Early Winter Spire (IV, 5.9 A4), and **Thin Red Line** on Liberty Bell (V, 5.9 A4), as well as the classic **Liberty Crack** (V, 5.11b A3).

The early ascents of many of these routes were made without the benefit of a trans-Cascade highway. If not for the proximity of State Highway 20 between Burlington and Winthrop, and the establishment of North Cascades National Park, this area would definitely not be included in this guide. As it is, many fine new alpine rock routes are being excluded from this guide, simply because they are "too far" from the road. Thus, although they have excellent rock climbs, Kangaroo Ridge, the Wine Spires, and Cutthroat Peak will not be found here. Perhaps in future editions of this guide, a section will be devoted to alpine rock.

A word of caution is in order here: unlike most of the other areas included in this guide, the Liberty Bell routes are mountain routes. These routes have additional objective hazards not ordinarily found at, say, Index or Peshastin. Many of the routes involve snow, whether on the approach or (surprise!) on the routes themselves. Most descents take gullies, which may or may not have snow and loose rock. If the weather is cold, don't be too surprised to find verglas. Rain, snow, wind — expect them all and be prepared. Thunderstorms may occur without warning, making the possibility of a lightning strike more imminent than at Darrington. Loose rock should be expected. Certainly, rain gear is appropriate on any outing here, and if you aren't certain of your speed on any route, especially the longer routes, it might be prudent to plan on a bivouac. Many a party has had to spend a long night out on a wall because they overestimated their speed and ability. So, while these nights out without food or warm clothing are usually quite memorable, if it doesn't sound like your kind of fun, be prepared. Also, if you are spending the night at the base of the peaks, bring insect repellent. You'll be glad you did.

Approaching the routes is fairly straightforward. The east face routes are best approached directly from the Washington Pass overlook, where a crude trail ascends across from the pullout (however, it is very difficult to approach the Early Winter Spires this way, as there is an obstructing buttress which cannot be passed easily). The west face routes may be approached from the Blue Lake trail, which begins from a pullout just west of the pass. A side trail breaks off from the main trail where the latter bends eastward towards the lake. The east faces of the Early Winter Spires may be approached via another "trail" leading from the parking lot at the sharp bend in the highway just east of Washington Pass.

While most of the attention received by the Liberty Bell group has been focused on the impressive East Face of Liberty Bell, which so far has three Grade V aid routes and one Grade IV free climb — including the classic Liberty Crack — be assured that there are worthy routes on the other peaks, too. Still, it would a fair estimate that 90% of the traffic here is on Liberty Crack and the Beckey Route. So once you have ticked those routes off your list, try something else.

South Early
Winter Spire

North Early
Winter Spire

Lexington Tower

Concord
Tower

Liberty Bell

The Minuteman

The B

LIBERTY BELL GROUP   photo: John Harlin

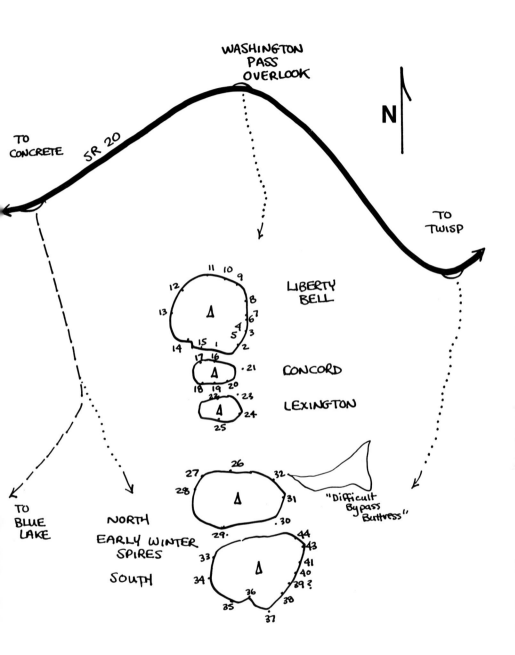

LIBERTY BELL OVERVIEW

LIBERTY BELL

Liberty Bell Mountain is the impressive, northernmost summit of the group, a classic bell-shaped dome with a striking 1,200-foot east face. That there is no easy way to its summit, and the fact that, until 1972, its only access was via a long hike, and as it is not the highest of the group (that honor going to South Early Winter Spire, which was first climbed in 1937) probably account for the fact that it was not climbed until 1946.

While each of Liberty Bell's faces has yielded routes, some free climbs included, its most impressive face has three direct, distinct Grade V aid climbs, including *the* classic of the area, Liberty Crack. However, despite its classic status (see *50 Classic Climbs of North America*), this route is not Liberty Bell's most popular route, that being the original 1946 route climbed by (who else?) Fred Beckey.

The rock on Liberty Bell is generally sound, and most routes follow distinct crack systems. Routefinding here is rarely a problem. Descents from Liberty Bell involve rappels down the approximate line of the Beckey Route, then down the west gully.

The routes are listed from left to right starting from the south notch (between Liberty Bell and Concord Tower) then counterclockwise around the mountain.

1. **OVEREXPOSURE**   ★ II, 5.7
   This short route begins from the notch. Traverse eastward on an exposed ledge, then climb directly to a tree above the ledge. Another 60-foot pitch reaches another obvious tree, then Class 4 leads to the top. Protection to 2"; bring runners. Rappel the route or the Beckey Route. FA: Ron Burgner, Don McPherson, 1966.

2. **FREEDOM RIDER**   ★★★ IV or V, 5.10d
   This is the first entirely free breach of the impressive east face. The route follows the obvious dihedral system left of Liberty Crack. After six pitches, the route merges with Liberty Crack for two pitches, then climbs Medusa's Roof (free) to the summit. Protection to 4"; bring comprehensive rack. TCUs helpful. FA: Brian Burdo, Steve Risse, 1988.

3. **LIBERTY CRACK**   ★★★★ V, 5.11b C3
   One of America's classic alpine rock climbs. This route climbs the continuous crack system on the left flank of the east face, and needs no real description. Follow the crack to the summit. This route can and should be climbed hammerless. Protection to 3"; include runners. FA: Steve Marts, Don McPherson, Fred Stanley 1965; FCA: Mark Gallison, Dave Seman, Steve Swenson 1974.

4. **MEDUSA'S ROOF**   ★★ V, 5.10b (5.8 A2)
   This intimidating variation begins from the ninth pitch of Liberty Crack, continuing up the more direct chimney/crack system through the obvious overhang. The second (?) ascent party climbed the route free, finding the climbing moderate by current standards. Protection to 4". FA: Hans Baer, Alex Bertulis, Mark Fielding Jim Madsen 1966; FFA: Brian Burdo, Steve Risse 1988.

5. **SOUTH FACE**   (−★) V, 5.9 A3
   A variation of Liberty Crack. From the sixth belay, traverse left to a sandy ledge. From near the left end of the ledge, climb up difficult aid cracks. A pendulum leads rightward to a long aid pitch, then up a long ramp and corner to a notch. Class 3 leads to the top. This variation has some rotten rock. Protection unknown. FA: Al Givler, Mark Weigelt 1968.

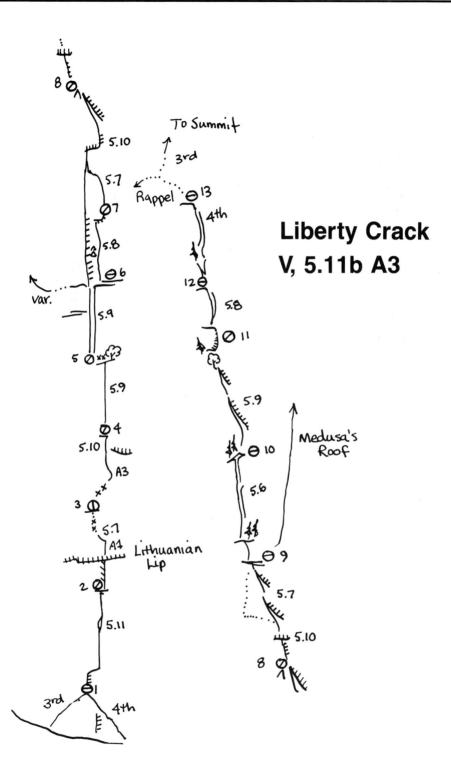

Liberty Crack

V, 5.11b A3

LIBERTY BELL – EAST FACE, LEFT   *photo: John Harlin*

LIBERTY BELL – EAST FACE, RIGHT   photo: John Harlin

6. **THIN RED LINE**   ★★★ **V, 5.9 A4**
Right of Liberty Crack is this long, technical aid route. Equipment to 3", including numerous KBs, LAs, hooks and small angles, plus many wired nuts. FA: Jim Madsen, Kim Schmitz 1967. Variation: The first pitch has a lefthand variation, climbing a left-slanting flake, then traversing right to join the standard route. This is reportedly a dangerous lead. FA: Tom/Mead? Hargis, Jim Langdon.

7. **LIBERTY LOOP**   ★ **V, 5.9 A4**
A variation start to Thin Red Line, joining that route after six pitches. Begin right of that route, at the lowest point of the face. This variation has several A4 pitches. In addition to the gear needed for Thin Red Line, bring rurps, bashies and hammocks. FA: Chris Chandler, Pete Doorish, Jim Langdon 1975.

8. **INDEPENDENCE**   ★ **V, 5.8 A4**
Another long aid route on the east face. This has eight independent pitches. Start on the right flank of the face and climb a dihedral and crack system to meet The Barber Pole. Finish via that route or Thin Red Line. Numerous to 4", including KBs, LAs, Leepers and hammocks. FA: Alex Bertulis, Don McPherson 1966.

9. **THE BARBER POLE**   ★ **5.9**
This route begins right of The Bong (a dark buttress directly right of the east face), and climbs exposed Class 3 to reach a long right-bearing ramp system. At the end of this system, just before the route meets a long left-bearing ramp system, are two variations. The lower variation stays with the ramp via thin liebacking (harder). It is easier to climb up, then right to a ledge. Continue leftward to meet Independence/Thin Red Line. There are several variation finishes possible. The free route climbs rightward across a slab beneath the Hercan roofs, then upward to the summit. Protection to 2", possibly including pitons. FA: Sandy Bill, Cindy Wade Burgner, Frank Tarver (by mistake) 1966.

10. **NORTH FACE**   **III, 5.8**
Begin right of The Barber Pole in a "red" gully. The route traverses left-leaning ramps to gullies and chimneys, which lead up to meet The Barber Pole right of the Hercan roofs. Protection to 2". FA: Fred Beckey, Ed Cooper 1959; FFA: Ron Burgner, Don McPherson, 1966.

11. **NORTHWEST FACE**   **III, 5.8**
Begin atop the broad bench above and right of the red gully. The best approach to here is via the south gully, although other more difficult approaches are possible. Climb an obvious chimney to a left-facing dihedral. Protection to 2½". FA: Hans Kraus, John Rupley 1956; FFA: Sandy Bill, Ron Burgner, Ian Martin, Frank Tarver 1966. Variation: From the large ledge in the middle of the route, traverse right to an obvious long dihedral and climb this. This variation apparently requires some aid. FA: unknown.

12. **WEST FACE**   **(−★★) rating unknown**
This route climbs cracks, corners and chimneys left of the obvious white arch on the west face. Because Fred Beckey describes portions of this route as "spurious," "poor cracks," "rotten gully," and "vertical rotten wall," it is probably not all that aesthetically pleasing. Take 30 pitons (?). FA: Fred Beckey, John Rupley 1958.

13. **SERPENTINE**   ★ **III, rating unknown** (not shown)
A crack/chimney climb beginning right of the white arch. The namesake crack is followed for two pitches to where an awkward traverse left leads to a more direct chimney. Protection to 4". FA: Fred Beckey, Doug Leen, Davis Wagner 1967.

Thin Red Line
V, 5.9 A4

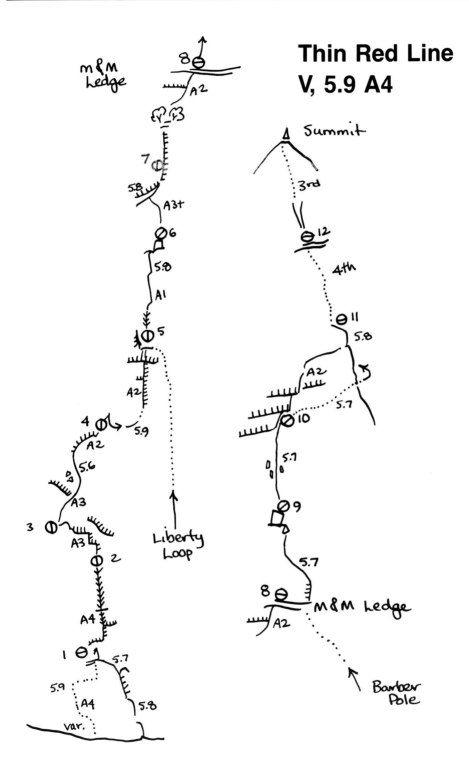

14. **SOUTHWEST GULLY   III, 5.6 A1 (?)**
The obvious gully, described for reference only. Possible snow and ice or verglas in season. Equipment unknown. FA: Donald Anderson, Fred Dunham 1962.

15. **BECKEY ROUTE   ★ II, 5.6**
The original route up Liberty Bell and still the most popular. Fred Beckey describes this as "400 feet of distinctly sporting climbing." The route begins some distance up the south gully, and traverses left across a ledge to a chimney. From the chimney's top, the route goes left across a "strenuous" traverse, then right (crux) to slabs and easier climbing. Protection to 4" FA: Fred Beckey, Jerry O'Neil, Charles Welsh 1946.
Descent: From the notch between the west summit spur and the true summit, downclimb as far as possible, then rappel from a tree. Another left-tending rappel (full 150 feet) reaches a small tree. The last rappel goes into the gully. Beware of the rope jamming on this last rappel.

CONCORD TOWER
Concord Tower is the sharp peak directly south of Liberty Bell. It is about as high as its "twin," Lexington Tower, but appears higher from some vantages. Descents are best made via the North Face rappel route.

16. **NORTH FACE   ★ 5.6**
From the Liberty Bell/Concord notch, climb a short, direct crack to a ledge. Traverse right, then go up cracks to the left. Continue left to a large block, then up a ramp to a notch on the left. A short crack reaches the summit. A variation finish leads up a righthand diagonal crack to the crest, then left to the summit (5.7). Protection unknown. FA: Fred Beckey, John Parrott 1956.

17. **CAVE ROUTE   ★★ 5.7**
Down from the start of the North Face route, traverse right across a ledge (past a tree) to a traversing flake. From a tree on the right, climb up and left to caves. Exit right to a long slab crack, then Class 4 to the top. Protection unknown. FA: Ron Burgner, Don McPherson 1968.

18. **CENTER ROUTE   5.7 A3** (not shown)
About 100 feet left of the South Face route, aid large cracks leftward, then up to the summit block. Protection unknown. FA: unknown.

19. **SOUTH FACE   5.4 ★** (not shown)
From the Concord/Lexington notch, traverse right to cracks and up. Protection unknown. FA: Donald Anderson, Donald Cramer, Bruce Schuler, Fred Stanley 1965.

20. **SOUTH FACE – EAST VARIATION   ★ 5.8**
From the notch, drop down (east), and ascend terraces to a large, obvious crack. Protection unknown (possibly to 4"). FA: Eric Sanford, Dick Sundstrom 1978.
Descent: Two rappels down the North Face route.

THE MINUTEMAN
This is the small spire on the east face of Concord Tower. It has one route. The descent is made via rappels and downclimbing on the Liberty Bell side.

21. **EAST FACE   ★ 5.8 A1** (not shown)
A six-pitch route up the outside face of The Minuteman, staying near the right margin of the face near the top. Protection to 2". FA: Scott Davis, Bill Lingley 1967.

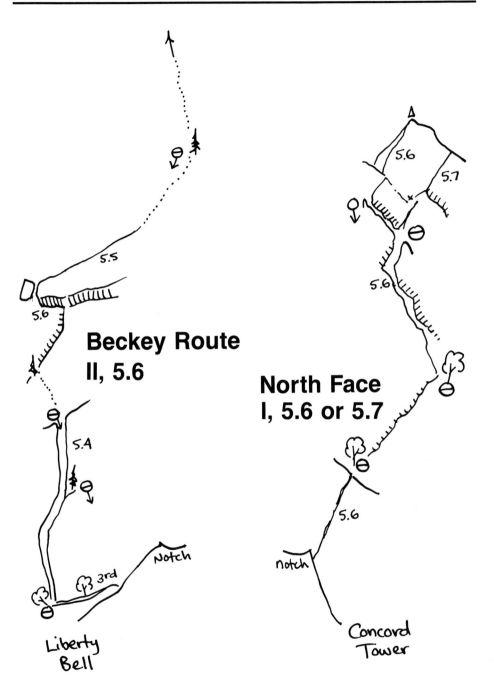

**Beckey Route
II, 5.6**

5.5

5.6

5.4

3rd

Notch

Liberty
Bell

**North Face
I, 5.6 or 5.7**

5.6

5.7

5.6

5.6

notch

Concord
Tower

5.2

caves

5.7

17

1

15

14

12

photo: John Harlin

LIBERTY BELL/CONCORD TOWER – WEST FACES

The Beckey Route, Liberty Bell *photo: Eric Sanford*

LEXINGTON TOWER

This is the second summit south from Liberty Bell. Best descent is unknown, although it is as likely to rappel into either notch.

22. **NORTH FACE   5.6** (not shown)
From the Concord/Lexington notch, climb a short crack to easier, broken rock. Obvious. Protection unknown. FA: Tim Kelley, Dick McGowan 1954.

23. **EAST GULLY   Class 5**
This is a gulley with a few moves around chockstones. Described for reference only. FA: Sandy Bill, Cindy Wade Burgner, Frank Tarver 1966.

24. **EAST FACE   ★★★ IV, 5.9**
This is a long free route which climbs through the impressive overhangs of the east face of Lexington Tower. Several moderate pitches lead to difficult climbing past a roof. A chimney, and friction climbing take one to the top. Protection to 3". FA: Steve Marts, Don McPherson 1966; FFA: unknown (Paul Boving?).

25. **SOUTH FACE   5.7 A1 (?)** (not shown)
A one-pitch climb from the south notch. Protection unknown. FA: Donald Anderson, Larry Scott 1964.

NORTH EARLY WINTER SPIRE

This is the northernmost of the two impressive, nearly identical spires rising above the other peaks at the south end of the group. The descent involves downclimbing south and west, then rappelling to the notch between the spires. A rappel from atop a giant chockstone leads to the southwest couloir.

26. **NORTH FACE   ★ 5.7** (not shown)
A pleasant route up the broad north face. Scramble up a brushy face to a short bulge, then up "steps" to a curving crack. Continue up a ramp into a chimney, then easier cracks lead up slabs to the summit. Protection unknown. FA: Greg Markov, Doug Martin 1976.

27. **NORTHWEST CORNER   ★ II, 5.9**
A fine route climbing through an impressive dihedral near the corner. Begin as for the West Face route, but enter the dihedral on the left via a thin corner and zig-zag flakes. Protection to 4". FA: Paul Boving, Steve Pollack 1976.

28. **WEST FACE   ★ III, 5.7 A1**
Begin on the left side, climbing an obvious chimney. Stay right, and climb up a long, curving crack system. Protection unknown. FA: Fred Beckey, Dave Beckstead 1965.

29. **SOUTHWEST COULOIR   ★ 5.8**
This is the "standard" route on the spire, and the line of the descent. Climb the couloir towards a giant chockstone. This may involve snow early in the season. Avoiding the chockstone is the first problem. The most popular variation climbs the left wall via a short slab, then traverses right on friction to the top of the chockstone. From the notch, continue on to the summit. Protection to 4". FA: Wes Grande, Pete Schoening, Dick Widrig 1950.

30. **EARLY WINTER COULOIR   rating unknown** (not shown)
The east couloir approach to the Early Winter notch. The route consists mostly of steep snow/firn, and the rock sections are usually aided. Provided for reference only. FA: Gary Brill, Lowell Skoog 1978.

LEXINGTON TOWER – EAST FACE   photo: John Harlin

NORTH EARLY WINTER SPIRE – WEST FACE

photo: John Harlin

31. **EAST BUTTRESS** ★ **IV, 5.7 A1** (not shown)
A long route up the prominent east buttress. The route begins some distance above a prominent dead tree, following a right-bearing ramp to the crest, then staying near the crest past overhangs, cracks and chimneys to the summit. Protection unknown. FA: Steve Marts, Don McPherson, King McPherson 1965.

32. **NORTHEAST FACE** ★ **5.7 A2 (?)** (not shown)
At the left edge of the ridge below this face, climb solid, licheny rock. Steep face cracks lead to a chimney. Protection unknown. FA: Fred Beckey, Joe Hieb 1958.

SOUTH EARLY WINTER SPIRE

This is the highest, and arguably the most impressive summit in the Liberty Bell group. This spire, situated at the southernmost end of the massif, has an impressive south face and east buttress. This was originally thought to be Liberty Bell by its first ascent party. Descent is quickly accomplished via the southwest couloir, although this route has some loose rock and possibly snow in early season.

33. **NORTHWEST FACE** ★★ **III, 5.11** (not shown)
This fine route climbs through obvious white overhangs on the northwest face. A left-facing dihedral and crux roof lead to steep cracks through the overhangs, then easier climbing to the top. FA: Paul Boving, Steve Pollack 1976; FFA: Boving, Matt Kerns 1977.

34. **WEST FACE** **III, 5.8 A3** (not shown)
This route begins in a left-bearing dihedral system and climbs leftward on slabs to a deep chimney. The Dolphin, a prominent prow/pillar in the center of the face, is reached via a deep chimney on the left. Largely unknown climbing. Take 48 pitons (?). FA: Jim Madsen, Fred Beckey 1967.

35. **SOUTHWEST RIB** **II, 5.8 A1** (not shown)
This route climbs the obvious rib left of the Southwest Couloir. Begin at a giant chockstone in the couloir and traverse left to an obvious crack. Continue up slabs and aid overhangs. More slabs, grooves and a crack take one to the top of The Dolphin. Continue left to the crest and up. Protection to 4". FA: Donald Anderson, Larry Scott 1964.

36. **SOUTHWEST COULOIR** **Class 3 (?)** (not shown)
Scramble up the obvious deep couloir past snow or loose rock. Provided for reference only. This is the standard route of descent. FA: Kenneth Adam, Raffi Bedayn, W. Kenneth Davis (?) 1937.

37. **SOUTH ARETE** ★★ **5.8** (not shown)
This is the pronounced spur immediately right of the Southwest Couloir. Mostly Class 4 with occasional cruxes thrown in for fun. Protection unknown. FA: Fred and Helmy Beckey 1942.

38. **MIDNIGHT RIDE** ★ **IV, 5.9 A4** (not shown)
This route begins at the right end of a narrow shelf right of the South Arete route. Climb into a vanishing "bottomless" crack. When it fades, move right towards an obvious roof and into a similar, left-leaning groove. A series of hook and shallow piton placements lead to a more secure crack system, and upward to the summit. Numerous to 2", including hooks and "special pitons" (?). Reference to Beckey's guide is appropriate here. FA: Henry Coultrip, Eric Sanford 1977.

39. **CHRISTIANSON-ROSKELLEY   III, 5.9 A3** (not shown)
An unknown route on the southeast face beyond (right of?) Midnight Ride. This route was reported by Beckey, but without details. Details are still lacking. FA: Bob Christianson, John Roskelley 1968 (?).

40. **CONSTANTINO-WHITELAW   IV, 5.9 C2** (not shown)
Another "unknown" route right of Midnight Ride. The route climbs four pitches up a shallow dihedral, and continues up corners past a large yellow block (some aid), then up a gully to the ridge crest. Protection to 6". FA: Duane Constantino, David Whitelaw 1977.

41. **INFERNO   III, 5.8 A4**
Another medium-length aid route on the southeast face, this climbing an obvious chimney system. A short pitch past a roof traverses into the chimney. Several pitches lead up the chimney to easier climbing. The crux is apparently encountered in nailing around a nasty off-width section. Modern wide-crack equipment would likely ease the aid difficulty. Protection to 2½", including rurps, LAs, and baby angles. FA: Steve Marts, Don McPherson 1966.

42. **SOUTHEAST FACE   rating unknown**
An indirect route which begins on the East Buttress route and wanders leftward across ledges on the southeast face. This is the original route up the face and the most inobvious. The route may be inaccurately shown on the photo. After two pitches on the East Buttress route, traverse leftward across cracks and ledges. Pendulums and rappels are involved, so good luck with the routefinding! Protection unknown, but some direct aid is likely. FA: Donald Anderson, Paul Myhre, Jim Richardson, Margaret Young 1965.

43. **EAST BUTTRESS   ★ IV, 5.8 A3**
An imposing line up the striking east buttress. The route climbs slabs from the toe of the buttress to a dihedral system identified by a prominent large block high up. From a ledge above the block, strike out right, crossing the ridge crest, to bolt ladders and crumbly aid. Equipment to 4", including KBs, LAs, baby angles, Leepers and hooks. FA: Fred Beckey, Doug Leen 1968.

44. **NORTHEAST CORNER   IV, 5.8 A1**
This route begins with several pitches of the East Buttress route before traversing rightward. A rappel into a hole leads to a rotten chimney. Continue up cracks and chimneys to the summit. Equipment to 2", pitons probably necessary. FA: Don McPherson, Steve Marts, Fred Stanley 1965

hole

SOUTH EARLY WINTER SPIRE – EAST BUTTRESS

photo: John Harlin

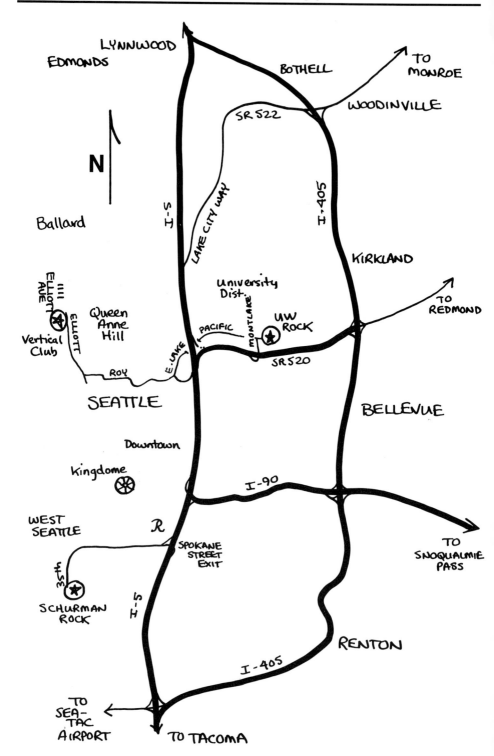

THE LESSER CRAGS

SEATTLE AREA BOULDERING

There are several bouldering and practice facilities in Seattle which are of interest to users of this guide. The most popular and well-known are Schurman Rock, the University of Washington Practice Rock, and the Vertical Club.

An updated, detailed guide to Schurman Rock and the University of Washington Practice Rock is in production. If you wish to obtain a copy, please contact the author c/o 4223 192nd Place SW, Lynnwood, Washington 98036. The guide should be available by summer, 1989.

SCHURMAN ROCK

Originally named Monitor Rock, this early artificial wall was built by the WPA during 1938 and 1939. The rock is composed of small boulders cemented together, and is intended to resemble an actual rock peak, with a main summit and a detached tower. The rock was renamed to honor Clark Schurman, long-time head ranger at Mount Rainier National Park.

The rock is located at the south end of a broad field in Camp William G. Long. The entrance to the park is located at the 5200 block of 35th Street S.W. in West Seattle. To get there, take the West Seattle Freeway up the hill and turn left onto 35th Street (at the first traffic signal). Go up the long hill, and watch for the Camp Long sign on the left. The park's gates may be locked after closing, which varies. Park regulations require registering prior to using the rock.

UNIVERSITY OF WASHINGTON

Possibly as an attempt to keep climbers off of campus buildings, in 1975 the University of Washington built its Practice Rock. While ostensibly for students and faculty only, the Rock has been adopted by Seattle climbers, students and non-students alike. It is the hub of Seattle climbing (during nice weather), where you can count on meeting friends and other climbers.

Rules for the Rock are posted nearby, and should be read and understood before anyone uses the facility. Most noteworthy, if you aren't a student, faculty member, or alumnus, you aren't allowed to climb on the Rock. This rule hasn't been enforced much, but proceed at your own risk.

The Rock is easy to find. Just locate Husky Stadium and you've found it. The cross streets are Montlake Boulevard and Pacific Avenue. The easiest way to reach the stadium is via Highway 520; take the Montlake Blvd. exit from either direction, and proceed north across the Montlake Bridge, and turn into the stadium parking lot as soon as possible. The gates are open after hours and on certain weekend days; otherwise expect to pay for parking. Carpool rates are the lowest, so bring a friend.

A word of caution for those who might try it: please don't place pitons or any other protection or aid device. Concrete isn't granite; it breaks very easily. Aid and leading practice should be undertaken elsewhere. Top-roping is encouraged for those desiring protection, but be mindful that if you leave your top-rope on a wall all afternoon, you are getting in the way of others. Move your ropes around so others can practice, too.

THE VERTICAL CLUB

The Vertical Club is presently Seattle's only indoor rock climbing facility. The Club's walls offer practice in slab, vertical, and overhanging face and crack technique, as well as fingerboards and free weights.

The Vertical Club is located at 1111 Elliott Avenue in Seattle, and can be difficult to find (especially in the dark). Once you are on Elliott, watch the addresses of the buildings until you are in the approximate neighborhood. The Club is on the west side of the street, with the entrance facing west towards the railroad tracks (away from the street). There is plenty of parking.

For one-day visits, the Club charges $10. Monthly passes are $35, 90-day passes are $95, and annual passes are $195 (cheaper than riding the bus). These prices are effective as of May 1, 1989, and are subject to change without notice.

In addition to training for advanced climbers, the Club offers basic instruction for those wishing to learn how to climb. The Club also hosts the "Spring Jam" bouldering contest each year. For information or directions, please call the Vertical Club at (206) 283-8056.

LARRABEE STATE PARK

Of the small bouldering areas in Washington, Larrabee is unique, as it contains a long, low shelf of Chuckanut sandstone along the beach to the south. The problems are varied, including face and crack routes ranging from 5.4 to 5.11. Among the more well-known problems is **Moonwalk**, a bucketed traverse involving several heel hooks, foot jams, and other odd contortions in which the climber's body changes direction at least twice. There are a few problems which should be toproped, however, so bring a rope if you intend to try them.

To reach Larrabee, find Chuckanut Drive (either south from Bellingham or north from I-5) and follow it along the water's edge until you find the park. It's easy! Refer to the map on page three of the guide.

MOUNT ERIE

Of the lowland rock climbing areas in the Puget Sound region, Mount Erie is one of the most unique. Located about one and one-half hour's drive north of Seattle, just south of Anacortes, Mt. Erie provides unique climbing on unusual rock. While most of the early routes (which presently comprise most of the existing routes) are moderately rated, there are several recent additions pushing toward 5.12. The climbing is uncharacteristic for Washington, especially the modern routes, which are pure, steep face climbs up vertical or overhanging walls. The rock is generally solid despite its dubious appearance. Just don't be caught off guard if you pull off a handhold by surprise.

Just as the climbing is unique to Washington, so are certain other features of Mt. Erie. As this is the only rock climbing area in Washington with a paved road to the summit (Index's Upper Wall and Punk Rock have roads to their respective tops, but these are not paved nor recommended for any but 4-wheel drive vehicles), it has the dubious honor of being the only area in the state where a helmet should be considered mandatory, at least on the upper cliff band. Even on weekdays, it is unwise to climb without a helmet, as high schoolers regularly "party" at Mt. Erie; the piles of broken glass along the trail should give climbers a clue as to what they do with their empties. On weekends, some of the dozens of tourists regularly throw items ranging from rocks and pinecones to beer and wine bottles off the cliffs.

Also, beware of The Mountaineers here. The club regularly swarms to Mt. Erie to stage its mock rescue practice, as well as beginning rock courses. On such days, the mountain is pretty much taken over, although it may be possible to climb on the lower cliffs without hindrance.

In deference to the wishes of certain locals, who have just begun to tap this area's limited new route potential, specific details of routes are not included in the guide. However, be assured that the author won't be so nice next time.

To reach Mount Erie, drive west from Mount Vernon to Anacortes. At the first traffic signal as you head north into town turn left onto 32nd. After several blocks, where the road jogs uphill and left, turn left towards Heart Lake and reach Mt. Erie after about three miles (signs point the way). A steep, winding road (Ray Auld Drive) reaches the summit. See the map on page three.

Be aware that the park closes at 10 p.m., and that it is heavily used by tourists, climbers and hang gliders. However, if the crowds and falling bottles get to you, you may hike downhill to one of the lower cliff tiers, which are rarely visited. A trail also reaches these cliffs from the east.

Those wishing to visit Mount Erie may wish to obtain a copy of Dallas Kloke's *Guide to Whatcom County Rock Climbing and Bouldering*. This, however, is no easy feat, as copies of this guide are rare.

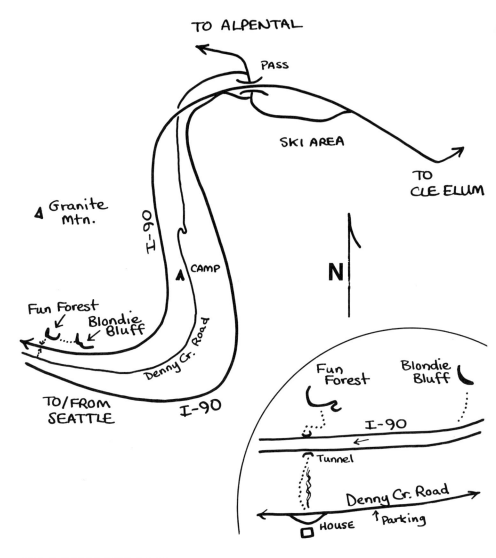

SNOQUALMIE PASS

The Snoqualmie Pass areas detailed in this guide are located along the lower south flank of Granite Mountain, and directly beside the freeway. That I-90 cuts so close to these small crags poses some problems, not the least of which is access. As it is unlawful to stop or stand on the freeway, except in an emergency, one cannot simply park near the crags. Another problem is noise. Try shouting belay signals over the din of the highway 100 feet away, and you will see — or hear — the problem. However, locating the cliffs from the freeway is very easy. See the map on page 36.

There are two main formations, located about 100 yards apart. Access is unusual. Take the Denny Creek exit, and drive northeast up Denny Creek road about one mile until you can see the Fun Forest crag across the freeway. Park off the road, and hike through a tunnel under the highway to near the foot of the crag.

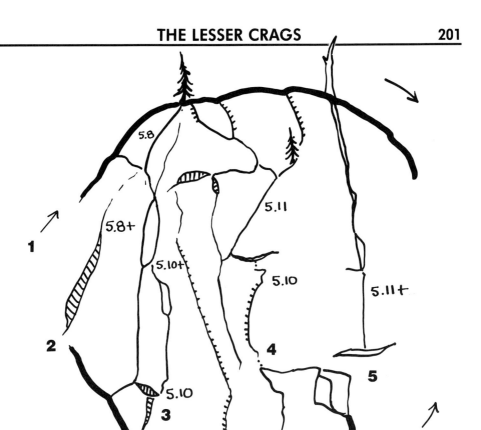

FUN FOREST

The Fun Forest, named for a Seattle amusement park, is the small, flat-topped cliff visible from Denny Creek road. It has several short, enjoyable pitches. Descents are made down the right (east) side.

1. **BOLT CRACK**   **5.7**   (not shown)
   The original route on the crag, a short, flaring, thin crack on the far left side. A bolt marks the start. Protection to 1". FA: unknown.
2. **TWITCH OF THE DEATH NERVE**   **5.8+ (R)**
   Right of Bolt Crack, and just left of Wild Mouse's arete, climb a groove to cracks. Poor protection. FA: Greg Olson (solo) 1987.
3. **WILD MOUSE**   ★★★ **5.10d**
   A fine pitch up cracks near the lefthand arete. Begins with a troublesome overhang. Protection to 1". FA: Jeff Smoot 1986.
4. **FLIGHT TO MARS**   ★ **5.11b (PG-13/R)**
   The obvious right-slanting crack in the center of the crag. Traverse ledges to arch and mantle to reach crack. Doubtful protection for first 40 feet. Protection to 1"; include TCUs. FA: Jeff Smoot, Hugh Herr 1986.
5. **VULCAN DEATH GRIP**   **5.11d/12a**
   The right-most crack. Thin, technical jamming leads to a dorsal fin flake, then easy to the top. Protection to 2"; take hangers for old, ¼" bolts. Frequently toproped. FA: Hugh Herr 1986.
6. **E TICKET**   **5.10c (TR)**   (not shown)
   Face climb on detached pillar. FA: Tom Dolliver or Nicola Masciandaro 1987.

BLONDIE BLUFF

BLONDIE BLUFF
    About 100 yards up I-5 from the Fun Forest is this small crag with two routes. Descend via ledges off the back.
  1. **TRAIN IN VAIN (aka THE SCARAB) 5.12 (TR)**
    The lefthand, curving crack. Possible to lead, but so far only toproped. FA: Dick Cilley 1984.
  2. **CLASH CITY CRACK ★★ 5.11b/c**
    The striking crack right of the prow. Thin, flaring. Protection to 1½". FA: unknown.
    There are numerous short (really short) routes hidden in the woods behind Blondie Bluff. If you have time, search out **Squirtgun** (5.11d) or **Ann With an E** (5.12a), both thin, arching cracks.

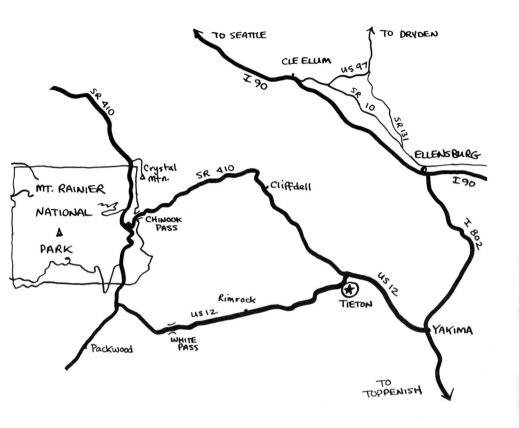

TIETON RIVER (YAKIMA)

With the growth in popularity of rock climbing, it isn't surprising that the excellent columnar basalt of eastern Washington has been discovered. While there are undoubtedly countless such crags in this area, considering the great quantity of basalt in the region (most of which is of incredibly poor quality), the Tieton River canyon, just west of Yakima, is currently the best known.

The climbing at the Royal Columns, The Bend, and Moon Rocks is typically basalt, similar to that found at Skinner Butte in Eugene, Oregon, with numerous moderate outings and a few difficult routes, mostly climbing cracks between the pillars, and rated between 5.5 and 5.10. So far, the aretes and faces have been spared the bolt, but it is merely a matter of time before these will be exploited to provide harder testpieces.

Those wishing to explore this area with more than the aid of the map included in this guide should refer to Matt Christensen's guide, *The Royal Columns* (1988), a to-the-point guide with a hefty price considering its size. Information may also be found in *Climbing* #110.

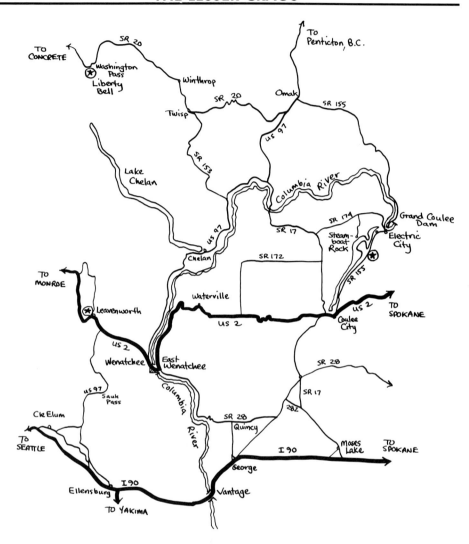

BANKS LAKE

The climbing at Banks Lake – near Electric City – has only recently seen some development. Located about 90 minutes from Wenatchee, this area usually provides sunny climbing when everywhere else is wet. The rock is granitic, and the area has much potential. Already, there are dozens of single-pitch routes up to 5.11 in difficulty. The principal problem with climbing here is that the routes must generally be approached by water, canoes being the favored vessel. Also, the area provides some of the state's most reliable ice climbing in the winter.

To reach Banks Lake (from Wenatchee), drive east on U.S. 2 to Coulee City, then head north on S.R. 155. The area is 16 miles north of Coulee City and eight miles south of Electric City.

Climbing #102 is the only printed source of information for this area at present.

ROUTE INDEX